THE
RACE CARD

THE

RACE CARD

WHITE GUILT, BLACK RESENTMENT, AND THE ASSAULT ON TRUTH AND JUSTICE

Edited by

Peter Collier and David Horowitz

FORUM
An Imprint of Prima Publishing

Published in Association with ICS Press

PRIMA PUBLISHING and colophon are registered trademarks of Prima Communications, Inc.

LIBRARY OF CONGRESS CATALOGING-IN-PUBLICATION DATA

The race card : White guilt, black resentment, and the assault on
truth and justice / edited by Peter Collier and David Horowitz
    p.   cm.
  Includes index.
  ISBN 0-7615-0942-9
  1. United States—Race relations. 2. Afrocentrism—United States.
  3. Racism—United States. I. Collier, Peter. II. Horowitz, David.
E185.615.R21226 1997
305.8'00973—DC21   96-52393
                                                CIP

97 98 99 00 01 HH 10 9 8 7 6 5 4 3 2 1
Printed in the United States of America

HOW TO ORDER
Single copies may be ordered from Prima Publishing, P.O. Box 1260BK, Rocklin, CA 95677; telephone (916) 632-4400. Quantity discounts are available. On your letterhead, include information concerning the intended use of the books and the number of books you wish to purchase.

Visit us online at http://www.primapublishing.com

CONTENTS

N early one hundred years ago, the black intellectual W. E. B. DuBois said that the "color line" would be the problem of the twentieth century. This was a daring prophecy at that time, for race was a sleeping issue in America, appearing only fleetingly in the periphery of the nation's field of vision. By mid-century, however, race and racism had indeed exploded into the forefront of America's consciousness, changing forever our sense of ourselves and our history.

The agent of change was the civil rights movement, whose moral passion and dogged courage brought down the malevolent architecture of segregation and legalized discrimination in just a few short years. The watchwords of the civil rights workers were "black and white together, we shall overcome!" Their commitment was to make the deferred dream of brotherhood and equality come true, and for one brief shining moment it seemed that America had stepped over the color line and entered a promised land of racial harmony and reconstruction. It seemed as if the future would be defined by Martin Luther King Jr.'s majestic vision of a world in which all people would be judged by the content of their character rather than the color of their skin.

But even as King was reaching the apex of his influence and the U.S. Congress was passing the Civil Rights Act of 1964 and the Voting Rights Act of 1965, forces were at work that would undermine this movement for integration and equality. Some of the opposition came from irreconcilables in the white world who had trouble giving up the old ways. But this group was an ever shrinking minority, out of touch with the mood of the country as a whole. A more serious challenge to King came from within the black community itself, where a radical fringe that had grown up on the edge of the civil rights movement developed into a movement for black power—an ideology of separatism addicted to theories of white guilt and "institutional racism," and to demands for reparation for black suffering. After his murder, King would be enshrined as the great figure of the civil rights revolution and one of the great Americans of the twentieth century, but the future belonged to those who wanted the color line to be etched permanently into the American mind and future.

Today, race is a more highly charged issue in our national life than at any time since the Civil War. Racial prejudice and bigotry, which were beaten back in the 1960s, have obtained a new lease on life, especially on college campuses, where separatism and group entitlements are the rule of the day. King's dream of equality of opportunity has degenerated into a vast race-conscious bureaucracy enforcing equality of outcome. The civil rights movement has ossified into a group of civil rights professionals with a stake in perpetuating hoarded grievances and a commitment to double standards and special preferences. Paranoia runs rampant through the black community, fully one third of which believes that the white scientific establishment has introduced AIDS into its midst. Instead of becoming progressively more color-blind, America becomes each day more rigorously color-coded. As reactions to the verdict in the criminal trial of O. J. Simpson demonstrated, blacks and whites disagree even on what constitutes reality. The race card, pulled out of a stacked deck of preferences and double standards, is played with devastating effect every day.

Never have the prospects of black people been better in America, and yet never has there been so much talk of race and racism. Moreover, much of the talk, even at the highest intellectual levels, is disingenuous, involving rhetorical guilt trips, hidden agendas, and verbal muggings. Attempts at candor are shut down by the eternal charge of "racism," which has become more often a way of invoking cloture on debate rather than a description of psychological pathology.

In this melancholy atmosphere, straight talk is a precious commodity. Rather than being divisive, it can lay the groundwork for a candid dialogue about a problem that shows evidence of getting out of hand. *The Race Card*, therefore, is an attempt to raise issues some would embargo and to investigate subjects others would avoid.

The essays in this volume originally appeared in *Heterodoxy* magazine, and some of them are heterodox to the core. In "A Death in Berkeley," for instance, investigative reporter Kate Coleman pieces together the circumstances that allegedly led the Black Panther Party to murder a white bookkeeper named Betty Van Patter who worked for the organization. In re-creating the circumstances of Van Patter's death, Coleman punctures the myth that the Panthers were a "civil rights" organization; she shows instead that they constituted a violent street gang, obsessed with guns, that had ridden the updrafts of sixties radicalism to a position of importance in the political culture. For a quarter century, Van Patter's death has been one of the dirty little secrets of the black radical movement. Not until "A Death in Berkeley" has this tragedy been autopsied and laid open to public view.

In "Free Mumia?," Paul Mulshine discusses how another movement spiritually descended from the sixties — the attempt to exonerate cop killer Mumia Abu-Jamal — sprang up in the nineties. Matthew Robinson's investigative report shows how government money has been funneled into Louis Farrakhan's Nation of Islam through contracts for guards who terrorize rather than protect housing developments in Chicago and other cities. And in "Afro-Fascism on the Rise," Ward Parks anatomizes a Maryland school district that was taken over by disturbing "Afrocentrist" theorists who remade the public school curriculum in their image.

The Race Card presents reports on people like Angela Davis, whose swift transition from an apparatchik in the American Communist Party and a winner of the Lenin Prize to the holder of an endowed chair in the University of California speaks volumes about the new dispensation of multiculturalism in higher education. It looks at Frances Cress Welsing, whose bizarre theories about black superiority have, as a result of the intellectual equivalent of affirmative action, worked their way onto the reading lists at universities all over the country. Another essay reports on bell hooks, whose eccentric lowercasing of her name is reflected in equally eccentric ideas about "institutional racism" that could have credibility only in the current inflamed atmosphere of racial hostility.

There is endless talk in contemporary America about race and crime, but "Black-on-White Crime" breaks new and melancholy ground. It is one of the first extended works to show the alarming rise of interracial crime and the degree to which racial animosity is at the heart of much of this violence. In "Slipping Through the Crack: Race and the War on Drugs," Cristopher Rapp takes on another hot-button topic when he attacks the myth that sentencing for drug convictions victimizes the black community in a conscious act of racism on the part of the criminal justice system.

Books didn't create the racial problems that have now come home to roost in America, and books won't solve these problems. But by taking an unflinching look at the hard facts, *The Race Card* proposes at least a partial answer to the question posed by the old Bessie Smith song, *What did we ever do to get so black and blue?*

—Peter Collier and David Horowitz

ONE

POLITICAL TRIALS

The Race Card

When it was revealed that Lionel Cryer, the male juror who flashed O. J. Simpson a black power salute right after the verdict in the criminal trial, was once a member of the Black Panther Party, the Simpson case finally found its context. That black fist called up a host of sixties memories, among them the ghostly voice of criminal-hero Eldridge Cleaver, who taunted the white world in his autobiography, *Soul on Ice:* "I'm perfectly aware that I'm in prison, that I'm a Negro, that I've been a rapist. . . . My answer to all such things lurking in their split-level heads, crouching behind their squinting bombardier eyes is that the blood of Vietnamese peasants has paid off all my debts." By the same corrupt reasoning, it is not hard to imagine O.J., his consciousness now raised to new heights by his new political advisers, thinking, if not saying, that Mark Fuhrman has paid off all his.

In the complex background of the Simpson criminal trial stands, in addition to Cleaver's hallucinatory voice and the gestural politics it spoke for, another trial that took place nearly thirty years ago and troubled the American criminal justice system even more profoundly—and permanently—than O.J.'s did. The defendant then was Cleaver's co-conspirator, Black Panther leader Huey Newton, charged with murdering a white policeman in Oakland. There was no question that Newton had been present at the scene or that he had threatened to kill a policeman in the past. There was a compelling timeline, a wealth of physical and forensic evidence, and even a black eyewitness to the crime. But as framed by Newton's attorney, Charles Garry, the issue was not whether Newton did it, but whether "the system" had conspired to put yet another proud black male in jeopardy. In putting the system on trial instead of the defendant, Garry joined up with the zeitgeist and invented the wheel that would be rolled adroitly by a generation of legal demagogues from William Kunstler to Leonard Weinglass. Garry's innovation and the radical racial themes he imported into the criminal justice system were part of an inheritance that ultimately passed also to Johnnie Cochran.

A young attorney with wide-lapel, lime-green suits and a luxuriant Afro, Johnnie Cochran was a sometime prosecutor, political fixer, and aspiring member of the Tom Bradley machine in Los Angeles during the seventies. By his own testimony, one event changed him forever — his decision to take on the case of Elmer "Geronimo" Pratt, a black Vietnam vet who returned home from the war with a knowledge of munitions and explosives and became the head of the Black Panther Party's underground "army."

In a case that would have almost eerie resonance with the Simpson affair twenty-six years later, Pratt apparently murdered a white couple in 1968 on a Los Angeles tennis court. Cochran entered the case and offered a defense based on the assertion that his client had been set up by FBI agents who had maliciously corrupted evidence and suborned witnesses. The theory did not play as well as it would a generation later when racial paranoia was more widespread and Cochran had a richer, more mediagenic client and a more immediately vulnerable enemy in the Los Angeles Police Department. Pratt was convicted, but the experience stayed with Cochran. He says that shortly after joining the defense team, he told O.J. about what had happened to Geronimo and pledged, "I will not let this happen to you."

Cochran could say this with some confidence because his own "life experience" (a term he told Oprah Winfrey he preferred to *race*) told him how deeply the radical thinking of the sixties had penetrated Southern California's black community, where racism— as his own meteoric career attests—is less onerous than at any other time in American history but is nonetheless an explanation invoked with an almost addictive fervor for any adverse behavior or social outcome affecting black people. A beneficiary of the changes of the last thirty years, Cochran saw how they could be used in the O.J. defense in a way that was not possible when he took the case of Geronimo Pratt.

Cochran learned, for instance, from Huey Newton, who had always insisted on white attorneys and juries. Newton knew that he could impress whites by his self-constructed political myth of the outlaw rebel, a man in "primitive revolt" against the social oppression exemplified by the guardians of that injustice, the racist police. This tactic was very successful. But he feared a jury of his black peers because he knew they would recognize him for the street hustler he was. Johnnie Cochran did not want O.J. to have a jury of his peers either. Brentwood millionaires would not buy the defense he planned to use to get his client off. He needed a panel representative of the black community, which he felt was now ready to believe the myth he planned to create—the myth of his client as a crossover artist who had taken his act into the white world but who had ultimately been rejected there, for all his charisma, because when push came to shove race overwhelmed even the power that comes from wealth and celebrity. Cochran was betting on the polarization and radicalization that had overtaken the black community in the last thirty years and so destroyed its center of gravity that it believed without question the notion that racism in America was worse than ever.

The system had been put on trial continually since 1967, most recently in the riot following the Rodney King verdict, and Cochran saw that it could be put on trial again in what, on the surface, was a less promising case even than Geronimo Pratt's. He knew the race card would trump the prosecution's full house of evidence. "Send a message," he urged the jury by the time he came to his summation — not "Seek the truth" or "Make justice prevail," but do the right thing and "send a message" to the system and to the LAPD, which is the system's most visible and most disgusting symbol. And Lionel Cryer's black power salute showed that the message — "It's payback time" — had gotten through. That this message hit home outside the courtroom could be seen in the representative reaction of Benny Davis, a black store owner in Los Angeles, who said after the verdict was announced, "Yeah, he did it. About time a brother got away with something around here."

If it is true, as Robert Shapiro says, that the race card was dealt from the bottom of the deck all during the proceedings that freed his client, it is also clear that the race card was played long before the trial began and Mark Fuhrman became the shadow defendant. From the outset, white officials in the Los Angeles County district attorney's office behaved like the character in *The Manchurian Candidate* who enters a state of mesmerized suggestibility whenever a Soviet control agent gets out a deck of cards. In the movie it was the Queen of Hearts that triggers this response, but in the Simpson trial it was the race card.

It was the threat of black riots like those that followed the Simi Valley trial of the policemen who beat Rodney King that caused District Attorney Gil Garcetti to file the Simpson case downtown — a world apart from Brentwood and O.J.'s life. This fateful decision, which more than anything else determined the outcome of the case, was followed by Garcetti's capitulation to a pretrial delegation of black leaders (including Johnnie Cochran) that demanded that the death penalty, itself a presumed symbol of institutional racism, not be invoked.

The race card was on the table in the district attorney's office when the prosecution left ten of its peremptory challenges unused and impaneled a jury with members who had been revealed during *voir dire* to be clearly sympathetic to Simpson. It is not hard to imagine what race cards were played when eleven jurors of color in the deliberation room finally confronted a sixty-one-year-old white woman who was a potential holdout.

This woman's daughter said afterward that her mother tearfully told her she thought O.J. was guilty and then added, "But Fuhrman!" And indeed Mark Fuhrman was like Voltaire's God: If he hadn't existed, Johnnie Cochran would have had to create him. If it is true that Fuhrman is a despicable racist with violent intentions, these intentions are probably no more violent than those expressed by O.J. in his repeated assaults against his ex-wife Nicole. The infamous tapes suggest how Fuhrman would deal with gangsters, crackheads, and lowlifes in South Central Los Angeles, but they do not predict very well how he would deal with a well-connected black millionaire sports legend in Brentwood. And in fact, when Fuhrman showed up at the Rockingham estate during one of O.J.'s earlier rampages against Nicole, he cut Simpson slack instead of taking him in, as he should have. Thus, for all the soundbites and fury about Fuhrman's racism, one might say that so far the only proven victim of his less than admirable behavior as a cop has been Nicole Brown Simpson.

Fuhrman's kid glove treatment of O.J. was a preview of the red carpet initially rolled out for him by the LAPD itself after the murders. At a time when it was supposed to be planning a strategy to "get" him, the police failed to identify Simpson as an immediate suspect and then left him free and unwatched—after notifying him of his arrest!—so that he could attempt an escape. Fuhrman might indeed burn all blacks if given half a chance. But the idea that he and his starstruck pals could have conceived an on-the-spot conspiracy to frame Simpson—a plot then ratified by the highest levels of the LAPD in the few minutes allotted—is about as credible as the notion that AIDS is a white plot against black Americans, that the government has a secret program that intentionally funnels crack into the ghetto, or any of the other lurid conspiracy theories that spread like a plague in the radicalized black subculture.

Johnnie Cochran's playing of the race card in O. J. Simpson's criminal trial helped accentuate the condescension and double standards that have come to distinguish discussions of race in America. Fuhrman's romance with the word *nigger* was treated as if it were the worst thing that had ever been said in contemporary American history. In point of fact, of course, slurs exist across the racial board. While Fuhrman's use of the N-word has stigmatized him and made him a hunted as well as a haunted man, for instance, the Reverend Jesse Jackson used the H-word (*hymie*, as in Jew, which is a word Jackson has occasionally uttered in public discourse in such a way as to make it clear he is forcing himself to omit the modifying adjective *dirty*), and yet he remains covered with honors, perhaps the most respected figure in the African American community.

There was also something fishy about the way the Los Angeles police were stigmatized in this trial. By the time the verdict was delivered, they were being routinely discussed as if they were the Gestapo not only by the defense but also by the media and the man in the street. In fact, far from being an Aryan monolith capable of implementing genocidal conspiracies on a moment's notice, the LAPD is 43 percent nonwhite with a black chief and a black commissioner. In 1994 the LAPD took 1 million calls, gave out 400,000 traffic tickets, and made 150,000 arrests. All this activity generated 139 complaints of "officer discourtesy" and 168 complaints of "excessive force"; of these, only 22 and 8, respectively, were found upon examination to have merit.

Johnnie Cochran's fantasies of living in a police state obscured the fact that in Los Angeles and other major cities in America, the issue is not lawless white cops but remorseless black criminals. It is not racism that has trapped one out of three young black men in the criminal justice system. It is not racism that makes black males, about 6 percent of the population, commit almost 50 percent of all violent crimes. If racism were to blame, blacks would not be the chief victims of black criminality, three times as likely to be robbed as whites and seven times as likely to be murdered. In Los Angeles County there are 1,142 street gangs, which account for much of the city's violence. There are many poor whites in Southern California. But of these gangs, 1,132—99 percent—are non-white. These young men of color control South Central like homicidal warlords, murdering people because they come from the wrong block, wear the wrong colors, or, like the three-year-old white girl whose family made a wrong turn in their car, are the wrong color.

At schools like the University of California at Los Angeles, scrawling an obscenity on the door of a student of color is routinely denounced as a "hate crime." The measurable and open hostility of black criminals to whites is the dirty little secret rarely discussed, but registered strongly in this chilling statistic: In 1994 there were 100 black females raped by white men, but 20,000 white females raped by black men, according to Dinesh D'Souza in his book *The End of Racism.*

Domestic violence, rape's distant cousin, is an important issue in this country—some 50 percent of female homicide victims are killed by past or present husbands and boyfriends. But it was apparently not an issue for the Simpson jurors, one of whom, the egregious Brenda Moran, played a subtle race card of her own in a post-trial news conference when she contemptuously dismissed as "a waste of time" the prosecution's effort to show that O.J.'s battering of Nicole provided a motive for the murder.

This statement and the visceral disgust with which it was delivered were so extreme as to invite speculation. Was this a black woman's rage at those iconic blonde goddesses like Nicole who are said to steal away black men like Simpson and Johnnie Cochran? Or was it the scorn of an African American woman who comes from a community where domestic violence is both routine and truly violent and who knows, therefore, what *real* battering is all about?

The Simpson affair has been treated as a great celebrity case in the tradition of the trials of Dr. Sam Shepard and Bruno Hauptmann, who was convicted of kidnapping the Lindbergh baby. This it certainly was. But it was far more a political trial whose antecedents are Charles Garry's defense of Huey Newton and William Kunstler's defense of Larry Davis, the drug king who shot nine policemen attempting to arrest him but was acquitted because Kunstler convinced the jury that the police had been out to "get" yet another black man who was only acting in "self-defense."

The real story in the Simpson case was not the defendant or even the defense attorney, but the jury itself. What were regarded as extremist slogans in the sixties (All black males are victims! All prisoners are political prisoners!) became the jury's key intellectual assumptions. The jury closest in spirit to the one that decided the O.J. case was the one that judged Lemrick Nelson, a black man who murdered a Hasidic Jew in Crown Heights in 1992. In this case, Yankel Rosenbaum was run down by a crowd of blacks chanting "Kill the Jew!" The killer was caught with the murder weapon and the blood of Rosenbaum on his person; he was identified by the dying man and confessed to his captors in jail. But taking the Garry-Kunstler-Cochran line of defense, his lawyers argued that Lemrick Nelson was the victim of a police conspiracy and frame-up. A jury of nine blacks and three Puerto Ricans acquitted him. Afterward, in their version of Lionel Cryer's black power salute, the jurors gave a party for the murderer to celebrate his release.

The Simpson jury could be sequestered from the public, but not from the resentment and blame that have spread through the black community like addictive substances in recent years. Nor could it be sequestered from the developing phenomenon of black racism, which feeds off paranoia and irrationality. It was no accident that the Los Angeles courtroom was filled with subliminal reminders of the tension between black radicals and the Jews who were their strongest allies in the heyday of the civil rights movement. Reminders of that inflamed relationship, which has come to be a barometer measuring the decline of race relations in America, were present in the appearance of anti-Semitic Fruit of Islam soldiers who functioned as Cochran's praetorian guard; in the fact that a Jew was one of the victims and that the verdict was read on the eve of Yom Kippur; in the bizarre neologism *genocidal racist* Cochran used to describe Fuhrman; and in Cochran's cynical comparison of Fuhrman and Hitler, which took holocaust revisionism to a new low.

By the time the verdict was read, Louis Farrakhan had become a ghostly presence in this trial. Initially, Farrakhan had scornfully dismissed O.J. as one of those black men who become trivial and inauthentic in their lapdog attempts to be accepted by the white world. (The buffoonish Simpson had once joked weakly that he could never embrace Islam because he liked bacon too much.) Yet, by the end of the trial, Farrakhan, acting through Johnnie Cochran, had in effect offered the defendant a safety net and a place to go when the white world of celebrity rejected him.

Transfigured by the racial solidarity that is now the highest good in the black community, the presumably sadder but wiser Simpson will now realize where he truly belongs. He will become a brother returned to the fold, a civil rights martyr, someone who might well show up as a celebrity figure at some future event like the Million Man March held in 1995.

And indeed, like the Simpson verdict itself, Farrakhan's march provides the mirror for a civil rights establishment so debased by radical strategies, double standards, and shameless appeals to white guilt that it has become an exercise in self-parody. (When Johnnie Cochran appeared before the Congressional Black Caucus and compared the Simpson trial to the Dred Scott case and the *Brown v. Board of Education* decision, there was not even a murmur of dissent.) Over the last three decades the moral voices of the black community were first muted and then drowned out, as dissent from the desperate search for psychological and fiscal entitlements that is now euphemistically referred to as the "civil rights agenda" was ruthlessly crushed. In the wake of the trial, writer Richard Rodriguez commented sadly that the two hundred years of moral capital stored up by the civil rights movement had been squandered to acquit O.J. He is only partially correct. That capital has actually been wasted incrementally all along the long march down the mountain—from the summit Martin Luther King achieved into the fever swamps of today—as racial hatemongers like Farrakhan and charlatans like Al Sharpton have replaced King and Medgar Evers; as lying delinquents like Tawana Brawley (who falsely claimed to have been abducted and abused by whites) have replaced true victims like Emmett Till (a black teenager brutally murdered in Mississippi in the fifties by whites who believed he had whistled at a white woman); as figures like the ever corrupt Marion Barry, the felon Rodney King, the thug Damian Williams, the cop-killer Mumia Abu-Jamal, and now O. J. Simpson himself have all been embraced as heroes of the struggle as worthy of admiration as Rosa Parks. This inability to discriminate right from wrong and heroes from perpetrators suggests that what now calls itself the civil rights movement has not only lost its moorings and its morality, but in some sense has lost its mind as well.

The system that Huey Newton put on trial nearly three decades ago has been attacked so often in the intervening years that its immunity has been destroyed and it is now prey to every exotic racial agenda that comes along. In the case of O. J. Simpson, black radicals got the payback they've been asking for since the days of Huey Newton. But its cost will continue to be paid—by all of us—in the years ahead. All during the year before the verdict, black leaders kept saying that O.J. couldn't get a fair trial. The tragedy of the outcome is that they were right.

True Lies

We're ready, we're ready, we're ready today," said Johnnie
Cochran in his trademark rapid-fire staccato. He was speaking to a supporter outside courtroom 107 at the Los Angeles Criminal Courts Building. "We're going to see if we can do it."

About an hour later, Cochran stood in the front courtyard of the
building surrounded by a gaggle of reporters and demonstrators, a
dozen microphones and tape recorders capturing his every word. "All
people who are interested in justice in this case are disappointed with
these proceedings. . . . It's outrageous, and nobody has the courage
thus far to stand up and say that. But we're going to keep on fighting
until he gets out. . . . I will not rest until he gets out. No doubt about
it." As Cochran ended his remarks, the chanting began: "No justice,
no peace! No justice, no peace! No justice, no peace!"

This may sound like an outtake from the O. J. Simpson trial, but
it's not. Rather, it is part of the continuing saga of Elmer "Geronimo"
Pratt, a man who could be called Cochran's *first* O.J., whose case
Cochran lost twenty-four years ago but refuses to let die. The case has
all the elements of the Simpson trial: a black man accused of brutally assaulting a white couple, racial and political rhetoric distracting
attention from issues of guilt or innocence, overripe insinuations of
conspiracy and cover-up on the part of law enforcement. And while

Cochran's maneuverings back in 1972 were not as silky as they have become, it was with Geronimo Pratt's case that he began to learn the language of radicalism that he used so effectively in Judge Ito's courtroom. Now, using techniques honed over two decades, he is attempting to get his longtime client a new trial.

In addition to the magnetic presence of Cochran himself, the movement to "Free Geronimo" has attracted a strange assortment of sixties nostalgia artists, Black Panther groupies, and leftover Lefties, whose common ground is the belief that Pratt was framed—by the FBI, the Los Angeles Police Department, and the racist "system." Pratt's story—potentially almost as cinematic as O.J.'s—is a disturbing mix of political ideology, historical myth making, and government foot dragging. As with the O.J. story in whose shadow it stands, Geronimo's case begins with the murder of a white woman.

The murder took place not in posh Brentwood, but in the more plebeian setting of the public tennis courts in Santa Monica's Lincoln Park. It was December 18, 1968, and Kenneth and Caroline Olsen had ventured out into the crisp evening to play doubles with another couple. When they arrived at around 8:00 P.M. they turned on the coin-operated court lights and walked out onto the court to wait for their friends. They weren't alone for long. Two young black men joined them on the court, pointing a .45 caliber automatic pistol and a .38 caliber snub-nose revolver and demanding their money, "or we're going to burn you." The men ordered the Olsens to lie face down on the court, grabbed a purse and a wallet from them, and headed for the gate. At the exit, they turned and fired at the prone couple, riddling their bodies with bullets. They then fled, leaving the still-conscious Olsens to die.

Fifteen minutes earlier, Barbara Reed had been sitting at the counter in the hobby shop she owned four blocks away from Lincoln Park. It was near closing time and she was writing Christmas cards and waiting for her husband to pick her up when two black men entered the store. One of them said he was looking for some materials so he could build a doll house for his wife. Reed explained that the shop had only recently opened for business and unfortunately was understocked, so she did not yet carry the things he wanted. When the men left, Reed locked the front door and turned the window sign to "Closed." A few minutes later, the two men were back at the door brandishing a gun and rattling the door handle, telling her to let them in. When she went to the back of the store to call the police, the men ran.

Barbara Reed's husband was waiting at a stoplight close to the shop and saw the men shake the door handle. When the light changed, he circled the block and saw the men hurrying down the street.

On a walk near Lincoln Park, Mitchell Lachman saw the Olsens enter the tennis courts. A few minutes later he heard shots fired and saw two young black men run away from the courts and speed away in a dark red convertible with a white top. The car had what looked like a North Carolina license plate. Then Lachman saw Kenneth Olsen rise to his feet and, holding his head, lurch his way into the Broken Drum restaurant across the street. Lachman followed him and together they called an ambulance for his wife, Caroline. Help came, but the damage had been done. In the hospital eleven days later, twenty-seven-year-old Caroline Olsen died of multiple gunshot wounds.

A month later, in January 1969, two leaders of the Southern California Black Panthers were gunned down in a shoot-out on the UCLA campus by members of Ron Karenga's United Slaves, a rival black militant group. Hoping to avert a retaliation, officers of the LAPD were sent to a house near the campus where several of the Panthers lived and maintained a stockpile of guns, ammunition, and grenades. One of the Panthers who lived there was twenty-one-year-old Geronimo Pratt, a decorated Vietnam veteran and munitions expert who would soon become the party's deputy minister of defense and the leader of its

Southern California chapter. Upon searching the house, Detective Captain Lucey of the LAPD found a .45 caliber automatic pistol.

Back in the lab, ballistics expert DeWayne Wolfer fired test cartridges in the .45 and compared them to the casings found at the tennis court. He concluded that they were fired from the same gun, "and only that gun." The striations on the two sets of bullets differed slightly, leading Wolfer to believe that either the gun barrel had been changed or the gun had been fired many times since its use on the tennis court.

On April 12, 1969, an officer of the California Highway Patrol pulled over the driver of a dark red Pontiac convertible with a white top for a traffic violation. A routine registration check revealed that the car had been purchased in October 1967 in North Carolina, had entered California in September 1968, and had been first issued California plates in March 1969. The driver and owner of the car was Geronimo Pratt.

Later that year, former Panther Julius Butler gave Sergeant Duwayne Rice an envelope marked "Do Not Open Except in Case of My Death." It contained a letter dated August 10, 1969, in which Butler claimed that Pratt had confessed committing the crime. According to the letter, on the night of December 18, 1968, Pratt told Butler that he and a companion named "Tyrone" were "going on a mission." Later that night, Pratt told Butler that he was nervous because he had shot two people on a tennis court, but did not know if they had died. When newspapers reported that a .45 caliber gun—the kind that Pratt usually carried—had been used, Pratt told Butler that he was not worried, because he had destroyed the barrel of his gun. Butler repeated these claims in court. In their testimonies, Kenneth Olsen and Barbara Reed also positively identified Pratt.

By the time—years later—that Pratt's attorney, Johnnie Cochran, had finished his defense of O. J. Simpson, many Americans may have had the impression that Johnnie Cochran had always been an international celebrity as well as the most politically connected attor-

ney in Los Angeles. But when Cochran agreed to defend Geronimo
Pratt he was still a wide-lapeled young attorney whose Afro ballooned
like a topiary and whose star had only just begun to rise. Cochran had
attained a degree of local notoriety a few years earlier in 1966 when
he represented the widow of Leonard Deadwyler, a man who had
been shot and killed by a police officer after a 90-mph car chase.
Deadwyler, intoxicated at the time, had mistakenly thought that his
pregnant wife had gone into labor and was trying to get her to the
hospital. Although Cochran lost the case when the jury determined
that the death was an accidental homicide, his polished performance
in front of the television cameras that broadcast the proceedings fore-
shadowed his mastery of the media during the Simpson trial.

But in the Pratt trial, Cochran's smoothness could not make the
jury forget the convincing evidence that connected Geronimo to the
murder. Cochran was simply outgunned by the prosecution, and
Pratt was convicted of first-degree murder on July 28, 1972, and
sentenced to life in prison. According to some accounts, Pratt did
not have much confidence in his relatively inexperienced attorney,
an assessment that may have been justified. At one point in the trial,
in response to the prosecution's contention that the murderer had
been clean-shaven, Cochran produced a Polaroid photo, apparently
taken in December 1968, in which Pratt had a mustache and goatee.
However, for its next witness the prosecution called a Polaroid
official who said that particular film had not gone on sale until late
May 1969. Cochran reportedly was "shocked and stunned" in much
the same way that the prosecution members in the O.J. case were
when a similar courtroom stunt, the pulling on of the glove, blew up
in their faces.

Pratt's conviction, which Cochran has called the "low point" of
his career, nonetheless functioned as an epiphany of sorts for the
lawyer. Before he met Geronimo he was a young black lawyer on the
make. But as part of his work on the case, he was "radicalized" by a
vision of America, the Panther vision, of a world that ran not only on

racism but also on power and political muscle. The experience that led to hard time for Geronimo liberated Johnnie Cochran.

Since 1972, Cochran's defense tactics have been displayed in a number of high-profile cases involving black defendants. In recent years, he has successfully defended football star Jim Brown (rape), actor Todd Bridges (attempted murder), and rappers Tupac Shakur (assault) and Snoop Doggy Dogg (murder). When pop star Michael Jackson was accused in 1993 of molesting a thirteen-year-old boy, Cochran came to his aid, orchestrating the estimated $20 million payoff that quieted the allegations. Shortly thereafter, Cochran told the press that Jackson had been accused solely because of his race, and that other blacks should beware, because "[if] they will try to do that to Michael Jackson, they will try to do it to anyone."

More to the point, as the O.J. verdict demonstrated so dramatically, Cochran's fantasies of rampant white supremacy fit the racially hypersensitive nineties to a tee. Over the years, the legacy of radicalism—for which Geronimo Pratt (veteran turned Black Panther munitions expert) is a perfect metaphor—has allowed the sweet-talking Cochran to convince juries to disregard incontrovertible evidence such as DNA because of "genocidal racists" on the police force.

It seems that Cochran did not draw the race card from "the bottom of the deck," as Robert Shapiro has suggested, but rather from the top. And it was Cochran's experience with Pratt that convinced him to play poker in the courtroom. In other words, preparation for O.J.'s defense began the day Geronimo Pratt was pronounced guilty. Cochran had learned his lesson so well that upon joining the Simpson defense team he told O.J. about Pratt's trial and vowed, "I will not let this happen to you." Clearly, Cochran—not to mention O.J.—owes a significant debt to the former Panther.

Perhaps recognizing this obligation, Cochran has never completely stopped working for Pratt's release. During a three-year stint as the third most important lawyer in the district attorney's office in the late seventies, Cochran sent a mailgram to the parole board recommending that Pratt be paroled. District Attorney John Van de Kamp angrily fired off a letter informing the board that Cochran did not speak for his office. Pratt was denied parole.

In all, Pratt has been denied parole sixteen times since his conviction, and four attempts to reopen the case have been rebuffed in the courts. A fifth attempt is being heard in an Orange County court now. Although Cochran hasn't been Pratt's lead attorney for some time, he has once again become a major spokesman for the former Panther, both in the courtroom and in the press. In the years after 1972, Cochran served stints in the city attorney's and district attorney's offices and also spent thirteen years as an appointee in former mayor Tom Bradley's administration. He has parlayed talent, political connections, and his personal brand of racial paranoia into fame and financial success. Pratt's conviction, however, continues to haunt him. "I can talk about $45 million in winnings," he told the *New York Times* last year, "but I still have to come to grips with the fact that Geronimo Pratt is still in prison, and I will not quit practicing until he's out."

Cochran may be closer than ever to collecting his gold watch. In 1992, James McCloskey joined the defense team. McCloskey is a lay minister and advocate for the "imprisoned innocent" who investigates the claims of people who are on death row or serving life sentences and works for their release. Although his efforts have sometimes backfired—shortly after McCloskey's findings helped to overturn his murder conviction, Benny Powell was arrested for brutally raping and sodomizing a UCLA graduate student and subsequently sentenced to fifty-two years in prison—McCloskey has had considerable success and has earned a reputation for tenacity. With his help, the defense team of Cochran and lead attorney Stuart Hanlon has built up a substantial case for reexamining Pratt's conviction, one that jibes in every detail with the racial rhetoric Cochran has been developing since 1972. Using FBI documents released under the Freedom of Information Act, police records, and the testimony of other Black Panthers, the defense team charges that Pratt was framed by the FBI, that the state's key witness perjured himself on the stand, and that crucial information was purposely hidden from the defense. In what must seem to him to be a sweet irony, Cochran has finally had an opportunity to apply the lessons that he learned twenty-four years ago from the Pratt case toward freeing Geronimo himself.

The FBI counterintelligence program known as COINTELPRO forms the backbone of the defense's claims. COINTELPRO was an attempt to infiltrate, monitor, and disrupt the activities of radical and militant groups like the Communist Party of America, the Ku Klux Klan, the New Left, and, in particular in the late sixties and early seventies, the Black Panther Party. According to FBI documents presented by the defense, a major aim of the Black Panther COIN-TELPRO was to sow factionalism both within the party and between it and other black militant groups and to discredit party leaders through smear campaigns, poison pen letters, and the like. COINTELPRO documents from 1970, the year of Geronimo's arrest for the murder, indicate that the FBI wanted to work toward "neutralizing Pratt as an effective BPP functionary." The defense argues that this raises the possibility that Pratt was framed.

The defense team also calls into question the credibility of the prosecution's star witness, Julius Butler. Butler may have had a personal motive for implicating Pratt; his letter was written only five days after Pratt expelled him from the party. More important, the defense claims that Butler perjured himself on the stand. During the trial Butler denied ever having worked for the FBI or CIA, but McCloskey says he has COINTELPRO records showing that Butler was an FBI informant from the summer of 1969 to the spring of 1972. Three members of the jury that convicted Pratt now say they would have voted otherwise had they known of Butler's connections. (*Note:* The district attorney's office would later lend some support to these charges, producing three confidential informant cards from January 1972 that the office had kept on Butler. Upon this disclosure, Butler characterized himself as a "reluctant witness," not an informant. The significance of the cards, the nature and veracity of the information that Butler supplied to the DA, and whether this issue has any bearing on Pratt's innocence or guilt remain to be seen.)

In addition, the Pratt defense team was infiltrated by two FBI informants who may have obtained knowledge about the defense's legal strategy. In 1981 the California Supreme Court, in a majority decision, determined that although informants had been part of the defense team, the information to which they had access was not significant; it decided that their presence did not affect the trial proceedings. Needless to say, Cochran, Hanlon, and McCloskey think otherwise.

The boldest claim made by the defense is that Pratt could not possibly be guilty of the murder because he was four hundred miles away in Oakland, attending a Panther Central Committee meeting, when it took place. McCloskey, joined by ex–FBI agent Wesley Swearingen, alleges that the FBI had wiretaps on the phones at Panther headquarters in Oakland from November 15 through December 20, 1968, and that wiretap records would confirm that Pratt was in Oakland at the time of the murder. When the FBI turned over its transcripts from these wiretaps in 1981, the entries from December 15 through December 18 were missing, and the Bureau explained that they had been lost or destroyed; the defense team maintains that these transcripts are the key to exonerating Pratt and that their disappearance is further proof of FBI malfeasance.

Although no members of the party spoke on Pratt's behalf at the trial, the defense team trumpets the fact that former Panther chairman Bobby Seale and former chief of staff David Hilliard now claim that Geronimo was with them in Oakland on that fateful day. And, as his trump card, McCloskey says he knows who really murdered Caroline Olsen. Police sketches based on Kenneth Olsen's descriptions of the assailants bear an uncanny resemblance to former

Panthers Larry Hatter and Herbert Swilling, both of whom are now conveniently dead. According to McCloskey, friends of Hatter and Swilling will say that before their deaths the two men confessed to the murder. Although this allegation is not entirely convincing, the defense team hopes it will add to the aura of suspicion that surrounds Pratt's conviction.

While Los Angeles District Attorney Gil Garcetti's office continued its investigation of these findings, Cochran and the defense team moved forward on their own, filing a writ of habeas corpus for the fifth time. On April 17, 1996, Superior Court judge Malcolm Cowell said that Pratt's request for a new trial "raised some substantial issues," but over the protests of Cochran and Hanlon he decided that he did not have jurisdiction to grant a hearing because an earlier petition had been denied by an appellate court. After reviewing the writ, the California Supreme Court decided that Cowell did indeed have jurisdiction and on May 15 returned the case to Superior Court. The hearing to grant Pratt a retrial is currently being held in Orange County. If Cochran and the defense team are successful, their efforts will lead to a new trial for Pratt.

The political implications of the case are obvious. Because the FBI, District Attorney Garcetti, the original prosecutors, and others associated with the conviction of Pratt refuse to speak about the case, the only information being circulated comes from the defense team, Pratt's supporters, and leftist groups wishing to push their own agenda. They portray the Panthers as harmless, even noble, community activists victimized by the authors of a sinister COINTELPRO program bent on genocide, a characterization in vogue among white leftists during the sixties and resurrected by the 1995 film *Panther*. Although their rhetoric was carefully crafted to appeal to guilty whites, the Panthers' modus operandi was typified by violence, drug-pushing, pimping, and brutality—all of which took place outside their white supporters' field of vision. By their own admission, the Panthers posed a threat worthy of the government's attention. Brian Sudan, Pratt's nephew and an organizer of the demonstration in front of the courthouse, describes the party as "a paramilitary organization," which would today be called a "militia."

David Hilliard, former Panther chief of staff, compares the party to the Sandinistas in Nicaragua and stresses that the Panthers were different from other activist organizations of the late sixties. He says that the fact that the party "talked about arriving at its destiny with arms, through revolutionary methods, and was in coalition with revolutionary peoples all over the world, certainly made us a threat to the United States of America."

And the arms the Panthers planned to use to achieve this revolutionary destiny were anything but penny-ante. In her autobiography, former Panther minister of defense Elaine Brown writes that the party's "most basic requirement" was that weapons be housed in every Panther-owned property. She describes in chilling detail the contents of the Panthers' armories. "There were literally thousands of weapons," she writes. "There were large numbers of AR-18 short automatic rifles, .308 scoped rifles, .30-.30 Winchesters, .375 magnum and other big-game rifles, .30 caliber Garands, M-15s and M-16s and other assorted automatic and semi-automatic rifles, Thompson submachine guns, M-59 Santa Fe Troopers, Boys .55 millimeter anti-tank guns, M-60 fully automatic machine guns, innumerable shotguns, and M-79 grenade launchers. There were suitcases, truck loads, closets full of pistols, such as Astra and Browning 9 mms, 45 automatics, .38s, .357 magnums, .41 and .44 magnums. There were boxes and boxes of ammunition, and large supplies of accessories, such as rifle scopes . . . and interchangeable pistol barrels. There were caches of crossbows and arrows, grenades and miscellaneous explosive materials and devices."

This listing, it should be said, reflects the Panthers' arsenal in 1974, *after* party founder and leader Huey Newton expelled much of the militarist wing of the Panthers and declared that it was "time to put away the gun."

Geronimo Pratt, whom the National Education Association has deemed "America's foremost political prisoner," was right in the middle of this. Part of his value to the party came from the skill with weaponry and explosives he had gained during two tours in Vietnam. This experience was what led him to become leader of the Los Angeles Panthers' military underground. When arrested for the murder in 1969, he was carrying a pipe bomb in his car. In 1970, he jumped bail and remained a fugitive for several months until the authorities apprehended him. At his latest parole board hearing, he was cited for six prison violations, including possession of drug paraphernalia and refusal to take a drug test. In fact, Pratt has given several indications that he may not be ready to reenter free society. For example, in 1994, parole board member Ron Koenig asked Geronimo if he would alert the police were he to witness a murder. Pratt responded that he would not, but that he might take it to "*our* law enforcement" (emphasis his). "I have a different reality," he explained. "You have your reality, I have mine." When Koenig pressed him on this question, Pratt said that Koenig had a "criminal mentality." Of course, none of this means that Pratt murdered Caroline Olsen, but it further suggests that he and the rest of the Panthers deserved law enforcement's attention.

Just as the extent of Panther violence and criminality is downplayed by those seeking Pratt's release, the size and scope of COINTELPRO is considerably exaggerated. Although supporters of the Panther mythology credit the FBI with "genocidal" intentions and a canny strategy that ultimately broke up the party, the facts of the Panther saga indicate that COINTELPRO brought out preexisting tensions within the party rather than creating them out of whole cloth. COINTELPRO engaged in fairly trivial, even somewhat infantile activity, primarily dissemination of poison pen letters, flyers, and comic strips signed with the forged signatures of party leaders. A typical message was the phony "press release" supposedly circulated by the Student Nonviolent Coordinating Committee (SNCC), a mainstream civil rights organization, in 1968. "According to zoologists," it read, "the main difference between a panther and other

large cats is that the panther has the smallest head." Other COIN-
TELPRO efforts involved anonymous accusations that certain party
members had venereal disease and cooperated with the police.

The evidence indicates that COINTELPRO was neither far-
reaching nor particularly successful. Hugh Pearson, author of *The
Shadow of the Panther*, the most complete and objective investigation of the party, says that the program "was for the most part a very
inept effort to sabotage the Panthers and a few other groups [that] is
credited by a lot of people on the left with doing more than it actually did."

In February 1971, writer Edward Jay Epstein performed a case-by-
case investigation of charges that the police and FBI were engaging
in "genocide" against the Panthers and found them completely
unfounded. "I think it would be a mistake to say they weren't being
harassed," he said recently, "but there is a difference between harassment and genocide." As for the talk of "genocide," Epstein replied
that "it wasn't [just] a case of being overblown; it was false."

On their face, the FBI's efforts seem almost pathetic given the
threat they were meant to blunt. Indeed, while the Bureau was sending comics and making prank phone calls, the party was stockpiling
weapons; disciplining its members with bullwhips; engaging in
prostitution, drug sales, and extortion; and literally getting away with
over a dozen murders. It would have been far better for the victims
of Panther mayhem if the FBI had been the powerful presence the
myth-makers describe.

But because these myths about the Panthers—part of the nostalgic
melodrama about the loss of the sixties paradise—are so persistent,
the claims made by the defense team have been accepted at face
value. Given particular importance are the statements made by
Bobby Seale and David Hilliard that Pratt was attending a meeting
in Oakland when Caroline Olsen was murdered. In fact, Seale and
Hilliard were silent about this alleged event for thirteen and nineteen years, respectively. Their newly recovered recollection of Pratt's

presence in Oakland on December 18, 1968, seems more like a conversion experience or an episode of recovered memory syndrome than a truth suppressed over the years by circumstances beyond anyone's control.

When I asked them about their tardy alibis for Pratt, Seale and Hilliard, not surprisingly, blamed COINTELPRO for their long silence. When the feud between Huey Newton and Eldridge Cleaver—which both Seale and Hilliard claim was created and exaggerated by FBI disinformation—reached a head in 1972, Pratt sided with Cleaver, and Newton expelled them both from the party. Newton then forbade association with Pratt in any fashion, including testifying in court on his behalf. In fact, the FBI had attempted to widen the gulf between Newton and Cleaver through poison pen letters and such, but as Hugh Pearson has shown, Cleaver and the rest of the party leadership were aware of the Bureau's presence, limiting COINTELPRO's effectiveness.

Moreover, both Seale and Hilliard were expelled from the party in 1974. Why did they not come forward then? Why did they let their comrade sit in jail for so long? When asked these questions, Seale recited his résumé. "At that time, we still had a lot of work to do. I worked fifteen to sixteen hours a day on various programs, going around the country speaking, et cetera. We more or less just forgot about it. I just went and got an advance to do my autobiography. I published that in '78. And then I went back on the lecture circuit, and then I worked on Capitol Hill."

Clearly, revealing the "truth" about Pratt was not high on Seale's to-do list. When asked if he thought it was unfortunate that Pratt sat in jail so long when his former brothers-in-arms could have helped to get him out, Seale became exasperated. "It's too bad that we had a bunch of ignorant, low-life, scurvy COINTELPRO FBI racists doing that shit. That's what's too bad."

Hilliard also seemed extremely defensive about waiting nineteen years to come forward. Pressed about this inexplicable behavior, he said ominously, "It sounds like to me you [are] working with the forces that want to create continued problems" and then declined further comment.

Walking amidst the picket signs in front of the courthouse at the Free Geronimo rally in late April, one realized how completely this drama from the sixties has been shoehorned into the racial clichés of the nineties. For example, Pratt's nephew Brian Sudan called his uncle's imprisonment "just outright racism," and Tanya Pratt, Geronimo's niece, said that he was in jail only "because he's a black man."

Others at the rally took the mythology to its logical extreme and seemed intent on using Pratt's imprisonment as evidence that their particular brand of revolution was necessary. A case in point was Hashim Rashid of the Minds of Melanin, a group that, according to its mission statement, is dedicated to the "liberation of Black People globally through the dissemination of facts and perspectives on Black Genocide, in order to bring about Universal Consciousness." Rashid said that America was an "oppressive society based on keeping black people down" and that Pratt's trial indicated the need for "revolution." When asked how this revolution was to be brought about, he chuckled, "I'm not going to discuss our operations with you. That wouldn't be smart, would it?"

The Spartacist League, a national Marxist organization, also used Pratt's court appearance to promote its agenda. Some of the signs carried by its members were particularly enlightening. One read, "THERE IS NO JUSTICE IN THE CAPITALIST COURTS!" Another urged onlookers to "FINISH THE CIVIL WAR! FOR BLACK LIBERATION THROUGH SOCIALIST REVOLUTION: SPARTACIST." A flyer put out by the organization explained that Pratt "has become a symbol of the racism which is the foundation of American capitalism."

The most verbose—and most entertaining—demonstrator was a representative of the Revolutionary Communist Party named Joey Johnson, who claimed to have been the defendant in the 1989 Supreme Court flag-burning case, *Texas v. Johnson.* (Johnson had burned an American flag on the steps of the Dallas courthouse in protest of Ronald Reagan's nomination at the 1984 Republican convention.) He praised Pratt for his "revolutionary principles" and for "making revolution in the heart of the Babylon madness, in the belly of the beast."

Johnson was particularly candid in placing the movement to free Geronimo within the context of radical revolution. Calling "what happened in Russia and China" merely "the first wave," he said that "it's not just a question of burning the [American] flag, we want to bring down the Empire for which it stands."

Next to these guys, Johnnie Cochran seems like a pillar of moderation. And while the truth about Pratt may never be known for certain, the resurrection of this case represents a homecoming of sorts for Cochran. In 1972 he lost the trial, but working with Geronimo convinced him that the key to legal success lay in massaging his own racial paranoia. Since then Cochran has been a Black Panther in a Brooks Brothers suit, speaking the language of radicalism so soothingly that listeners often don't hear what he's saying. Spurred on by the memory of Pratt's conviction and using the lessons of 1972, Cochran orchestrated his greatest victory in the O.J. trial. Now, having rehearsed his lines for two decades, he returns to Geronimo's side.

The basic scenario presented by the defense—a black man accused of killing a white woman, with allegations of prosecutorial irregularities and a law enforcement conspiracy—is one that Cochran has now worked out to perfection. Whether or not it works for Geronimo is yet to be determined, but Cochran does seem to be in his element, as this case seems tailor-made for him now that his own ability and the temper of the times are in a harmonic convergence. All of the roles made famous by the O.J. trial are here: the long-imprisoned Pratt as O.J., J. Edgar Hoover in the Mark Fuhrman role, Bobby Seale and David Hilliard as the slightly embarrassing Kato Kaelin, the demonstrators as themselves, and the maestro Cochran himself ready to reprise his role as a hip black version of Clarence Darrow. All that is lacking are the camera and the courtroom, two things that could well fit Johnnie's first O.J. like a glove.

Free Mumia?

Several years after the murder of her husband, Maureen
Faulkner moved to Southern California. It was as complete a
change as she could imagine, from the confined rowhouse neighborhoods of Philadelphia to the wide-open beaches of the Pacific.
She wanted to get away from it all, but the horror of his death has
followed her.

"I had a very interesting experience the other day," she told me. "I
was pumping gas and I saw this guy get out of his car and he had on
a 'Free Mumia' T-shirt. I went over to him and I said, 'Excuse me.
Where did you get that shirt?'

"'At a rally at UCLA,' he said.

"'Tell me about the case,' I said.

"'It's about a Black Panther and the police framed him,' he said.

"I said, 'Who do you really think shot the cop?'

"'Some other guy did it and ran away,' he said.

"I said, 'You better get your facts straight, because the next time
you walk around wearing a shirt like that the widow of the officer
may come up to you.'

"He said, 'You mean you're the widow?'

"I said, 'If you give me your name and address, I'll send you the
facts of the case.'

"He said, 'No, thanks.'"

Maureen Faulkner wasn't surprised by this response. Those who worship in the cult of Mumia Abu-Jamal are allergic to the facts. In fact, ignorance is a precondition for the religious experience. Far better to restrict oneself to the experience of Jamal's cuddly image as an existential dreadlocked intellectual and of his voice, a wonderful, mellifluous instrument familiar to listeners of National Public Radio's *All Things Considered*. In a gesture reminiscent of the Ayatollah's communiqués from Paris during the years of his exile, Jamal regularly sends out from death row cassettes that reach the hands of the faithful in faraway places.

In Pennsylvania, where people know about him, Jamal is a nonentity, but in California he's a star. TV actors like Ed Asner and Mike Farrell preach his gospel. And college students in Los Angeles wear T-shirts emblazoned with his image and reject any invitation to learn the facts about his case.

The University of California has done some amazing things over the years, but perhaps its most remarkable accomplishment has been to make available to the masses the sort of high-minded ignorance that used to be the sole province of Ivy League alumni. It produces an amazing type of person, superficially educated yet totally devoid of the type of intellectual curiosity that the university education is supposed to engender.

When I covered the wars in Central America in the 1980s, I was amazed at the number of University of California students I'd run into in places like Nicaragua and Guatemala. I'd hear these people making huge, sweeping statements about local politics that had absolutely no basis in fact. I'd offer to show them some writings and documents that might alter their views, but they—like the guy Maureen Faulkner met in the gas station—would decline. Thought to them was not a matter of dry facts and boring theories; it was a question of consciousness. Once one's consciousness was raised about a given question, that was that.

Though I grew up and live in the East, I attended the University of California in the 1960s, so I'm not unaware of the roots of this phenomenon. It's what could be called the California Fallacy: that high moral authority derives from living in a beautiful place. When you're up in the eucalyptus groves above Berkeley, gazing at a panorama of the San Francisco Bay and the Pacific Ocean beyond, it's easy to believe that your thoughts are as wonderful as the view. This isn't true, but it has one major advantage from my point of view: Practitioners of the California Fallacy rarely show up where I live, just outside Philadelphia.

So it was a bit of a shock when, upon emerging from the dingy, gray Philadelphia courtroom in which the case of Mumia Abu-Jamal was being argued, I found myself surrounded by a handful of University of California types who had caravanned east to chant on behalf of their favorite political prisoner. It was only a little more shocking when—fifteen minutes later—I was being assaulted by two of them on the street in broad daylight.

But I'm getting ahead of myself. I was at the hearing in August 1995 because I was trying to discover just what it is about Jamal that has made him into an international celebrity. His fame is certainly a mystery to the working journalists of Philadelphia who have covered his case since the beginning. The evidence against Jamal at his trial was so conclusive that no one, not even those who are Philadelphia's politically liberal equivalent of the conservative, wealthy Main Line residents, doubts that Jamal shot police officer Daniel Faulkner.

One of the journalists who knows the case best is David Holmberg, who covered it for the *Philadelphia Daily News*. At the time of the trial in 1982, he was a committed liberal who was very skeptical of the Philadelphia police. He was prepared to give Jamal the benefit of the doubt. "It was just one of those things where the whole tone was, hey, this is a black guy. This is the Philadelphia police. If you were there at the time, your first inclination was to identify with Jamal," says Holmberg. "But the evidence was just so overwhelming. The testimony was so convincing."

Not only that, but Jamal also sabotaged his own defense by demanding to act as his own attorney. The crusty old judge, Albert

Sabo, granted that request but refused to grant a further request—
that Jamal be aided in his defense by John Africa, leader of a weird
back-to-nature cult called MOVE that Jamal had embraced.
Mumia's ties with the cult had become so strong, in fact, that he had
left his part-time job as a correspondent for public radio. Although
in late 1981, the time of the killing, Jamal was the head of the local
chapter of the National Association of Black Journalists, by then he
had only a tenuous connection to the journalism profession. He
made his living by driving a cab.

When Judge Sabo refused to permit John Africa to join the defense
team, Jamal responded by disrupting the trial and playing to the audience, which was composed largely of MOVE members. A pattern
developed. After warning him several times to cease disrupting the
proceedings, Sabo would have Jamal removed from the courtroom
and let his backup attorney, Anthony Jackson, handle the defense.
Then Jamal would return for a while, until his next disruption.

After the jury returned a guilty verdict on first-degree murder,
Jamal sealed his fate by choosing to address the jury during the
penalty phase. He began a long political harangue during which he
openly insulted the jurors, two of whom were black. They responded
by sentencing him to death. Jamal's behavior was so bizarre that a
Philadelphia Inquirer reporter speculated in print that the defendant
was suicidal.

David Holmberg, now with a Florida newspaper, says he can't
understand how the pathetic character on display at the trial meta-
morphosed into the cult hero of an international movement. "It's
amazing the way these people come out of the woodwork for
Mumia," he says.

That's what I figured and that's why I was in the courtroom
when Jamal was brought into Philadelphia for hearings on the
appeal of his death sentence. I wanted to find out just who was behind the Mumia phenomenon. One day, after the hearing ended,
I went into the plaza to interview the demonstrators who'd
been showing up faithfully for several weeks. A rather pleasant-

looking young woman handed me a "Free Mumia" pamphlet. I asked if I could interview her. It began well enough. She gave her name as Karla and her age as twenty-three. A graduate of the University of California, Santa Cruz, she was looking for something to do during the summer, so she joined a six-car "caravan for justice" that began in Santa Cruz and eventually brought twenty-seven people to Philadelphia. She was a very nice, very sincere person who—in the great University of California tradition—was innocent of any knowledge of the case that she had traveled three thousand miles to protest.

I knew a lot more about the case than she did, and not simply because I'm a journalist. By pure coincidence I happened to be what might be called an "earwitness" to the crime. On December 9, 1981, I was living just two blocks from 13th and Locust streets in Philadelphia. I was up late that night writing. I was still awake when, just before 4:00 A.M., I heard a quick burst of what sounded like gunfire. I heard five or six shots, and it was over almost as soon as it began. Then I heard sirens.

The next morning, the newspapers said that a twenty-five-year-old cop by the name of Daniel Faulkner had been shot to death. Jamal was also shot, apparently by the cop. The facts were not controversial. Faulkner had stopped Jamal's brother, William Cook, for a traffic violation. Jamal happened, by what appears to have been pure coincidence, to have been driving a cab nearby. He observed Faulkner and Cook struggling. He ran across the street toward them and shot Faulkner in the back, according to the police account. Faulkner got off one shot and hit Jamal in the chest. Jamal then stood over the fallen officer and fired four more shots. When police arrived on the scene they found Faulkner dying from a bullet between the eyes and Jamal sitting on a curb nearby. A .38 caliber Charter Arms revolver registered to Jamal was at his feet with five spent cartridges in it. Jamal was wearing a holster.

I asked Karla to explain to me how Jamal could possibly have been innocent. Why was he wearing a holster? What happened to

Jamal's five bullets? Had he, in a burst of compassion, fired them into the air while some Good Samaritan came to his aid and shot the officer?

"I don't know," Karla said. "There's a big possibility that another person shot him."

"Give me a scenario," I said. "Just one."

At this point she became a bit confused. She fetched another Mumiaite. He gave his name as Dan.

"Did you graduate from UCSC?" I asked.

"I went there," he said.

"Give me a scenario."

"There's a lot of scenarios," he said. "There were 125 eyewitnesses who claim they saw what happened, and the defense didn't get a chance to question them."

"Wait a minute," I said. "One hundred and twenty-five eye-witnesses at Broad and Locust at 4:00 A.M. on a December night? Have you ever been to Broad and Locust?"

Dan admitted he hadn't. I pointed out to him that, having traveled three thousand miles, he might want to walk three blocks to visit the murder scene. This might aid him in realizing that the intersection of Broad and Locust was certainly not the type of place where hundreds of people congregate at 4:00 A.M.

He backpedaled: "I'm not saying 125 people saw who did what."

"What are you saying? You mean you came all this distance and you've never even thought of a scenario by which your man could possibly be innocent?"

At this point Dan and Karla seemed to realize that, unlike most of the out-of-town journalists who had descended on Philadelphia for the Jamal hearings, I was not a fan.

"I don't want you to quote me," said Karla. "I want my quotes back."

"I'll consider it," I said.

"Me too," said Dan. "I don't want you to quote me."

I began to walk away. The City Hall courtyard was filled with Mumiaites, and I didn't want to attract a crowd of them. They were the usual collection of clueless Quakers, burned-out sixties radical women, and rasta-dressed middle-class black people. They'd been having their little party out there for days, and it was a pathetic sight. A woman who identified herself as the Socialist candidate for New York City Council took the megaphone to praise Cuba as "the only revolutionary free nation on the earth." At another point, a young black man who might have been a college student actually smashed a black-and-white TV with a crowbar to show his contempt for the media. I hadn't the heart to tell him that that particular piece of guerrilla theater had become a cliché before he was born.

No, I didn't want to get mau-maued by that crew. So I tucked my notebook in my back pocket and melted into the midday crowd. It was when I was a block away from City Hall that it happened. I felt a tug. I turned and saw Karla trying to escape with my notebook. I grabbed it back. Karla, to give credit where it's due, had a hell of a strong grip. Before I could work my notebook free, I felt someone grabbing me from behind. It was a tall Jamal supporter whom I'd seen back at City Hall. "Call the police!" I began to yell at bystanders.

The thought of an imminent arrest by the Philadelphia police instantly inspired a burst of rationality in the Mumiaites. The tall guy let go, and Karla surrendered the notebook. I stuck my finger in the tall guy's chest. "Listen, bozo, I could have you arrested for assault!"

"I am not a bozo!" he replied.

"Can't we compromise?" said Karla. "Those are my quotes. I don't want them used."

"Well, if you don't want your quotes used, don't talk to journalists," I told her. "This is the East. We play for keeps."

I went looking for a pay phone to dial 911 and have the two arrested. But by the time I found one, I began to appreciate the humor in the incident. "I am not a bozo!"—they should print that up on the back of all those T-shirts that say "Free Mumia!" in front.

The next night I attended a panel discussion on the Jamal case. By coincidence, the annual convention of the National Association of Black Journalists was in town. Security was heavy. The Mumiaites were out in force, picketing at the entrance to the hotel where the convention was being held. The panel featured attorneys on opposite sides of the case. For Jamal, there was Leonard Weinglass, the left-wing lawyer who has represented everyone from the Chicago Seven to the men who bombed the World Trade Center. The anti-Jamal side was represented by Joseph McGill, who had prosecuted Jamal in the original trial in 1982. McGill had since left the district attorney's office and gone into private practice, but he retained an interest in the Jamal case. He was fond of telling the media that the case was a prosecutor's dream, with every base covered—from motive to physical evidence to eyewitness testimony.

The panel discussion promised great drama, tremendous tension. The room was packed with the cream of the nation's black journalists, hundreds of reporters and editors from all over the country who were eager to examine the racially charged case of a black journalist on death row for killing a white policeman in a city that had had a history of bad relations between the races. As it began, the principals fiddled with their microphones and talked nervously.

Then an amazing thing happened—nothing. Weinglass got a bit of a charge out of the audience by bringing up every possible racial aspect of the case. He hit hard on the idea that the Philadelphia police were out to get Jamal because he had been a Black Panther in his youth. But McGill pointed out the simple facts of the case. Even if the police had been out to get Jamal, there is no way they could have arranged for him to show up at that particular intersection, armed, at the exact moment his brother was being arrested.

"It is almost beyond belief to imagine a conspiracy so wide and so deep as to get all this evidence together," McGill said. He pointed out that the defense had failed to come up with any challenge to the fact that Jamal's gun was found at his feet with five spent casings in it.

As for Jamal's political involvement, it was more likely to prove his guilt than his innocence, McGill argued. Jamal's obsession with the MOVE cult had led him to grow dreadlocks and become an advocate of the group, if not a member. Shortly before the Faulkner shooting, Jamal had covered a trial at which MOVE members were convicted of killing a white policeman during a siege at one of their fortified houses. "Abu-Jamal indicated he was just overwhelmed with anger in 1981 when the MOVE members were sentenced," said McGill.

Shortly after this statement I first noticed a curious phenomenon: The black journalists in the audience were filing out. Discreetly, in ones and twos, they began making their way to the back of the room. Elsewhere in the hotel were hospitality suites, recruiters from major newspapers, all kinds of attractions for the young, well-dressed, upwardly mobile cream of the African American journalistic establishment. Inside was a debate between white people about what, when you got right down to it, was the sort of local crime story that most reporters have seen enough of.

The question-and-answer session began. A Jamal supporter, one of those aging-hippie types with long hair on the sides but none on top, began a tirade on the subject of how unfair it was to call Jamal a "convicted cop-killer." This characterized Jamal as someone who habitually killed police officers, when, in fact, he was accused of having done it only once. The moderator cut him off after a minute or so: "Do you have a question?"

"Yes," the man said. "Mr. McGill, how can you call Mumia Abu-Jamal a cop-killer?"

"He killed a cop," McGill replied.

"That doesn't make him a cop-killer!" the guy yelled.

This dialogue caused the remaining black journalists to look at each other. The movement toward the doors became less discreet. There were still some unfortunates left, however, when Pam Africa got to the microphone. She had wild dreadlocks and a child, also in dreadlocks, on her hip. The assembled black journalists seemed appalled. Unlike us white male journalists, who generally dress only slightly better than carpenters, black journalists tend to have a sense of style. Pam Africa was a living stereotype of every upwardly mobile black professional's nightmare.

In a guttural voice, Ms. Africa began a tirade on the innocence of Jamal. The trickle to the exits became a flood. After the panel discussion ended, a few black journalists whom I knew came over and discussed the Jamal case with me. They knew I was covering the case, and they were being polite. But to them, it was a nonstory.

And for good reason. Leonard Weinglass has done an admirable job of fooling the national media into thinking there is some doubt about who shot Faulkner. But he's up against a problem often cited by a football coach at my old high school: You can't make chicken salad out of chicken shit. Jamal's decision to act as his own attorney at his 1982 trial left Weinglass with a trial record that is extremely damaging to his client. Weinglass can nibble at the edges of the evidence all he wants, but he can't get rid of that Charter Arms revolver found at Mumia Abu-Jamal's feet. Weinglass concedes there were five spent casings in the gun, but he criticizes the police for not testing the gun to see if it had been fired recently.

"How do you do that?" someone asked. Weinglass said, "You just smell it."

Wonderful: His client was literally caught with a smoking gun, so he criticizes the police for not smelling the smoke.

The other objections raised by Weinglass and the Jamal supporters have little coherence. The objections represent at least four separate and mutually exclusive theories of what happened that night. The theories get more and more fantastic as the case progresses. In this latest hearing, the defense one day produced a witness who said Faulkner was shot by a passenger in William Cook's car and on another day produced a witness who said Faulkner was shot by a guy with "Johnny Mathis hair" who drove up to the scene in the middle of the action and fired the coup de grâce into Faulkner's face.

The press reported these scenarios as if they might have had validity. This is nonsense. The media have—amazingly—failed to report the most salient fact about the Jamal case: Jamal has never once said he didn't shoot Faulkner. A *Time* magazine article, for example, repeated the oft-stated contention that Jamal has denied shooting Faulkner. But in fact, he's never made such a statement. At his trial, he divided his time between political tirades about the MOVE organization and questioning that seemed to indicate a mild endorsement of the mystery-gunman theory. This strategy backfired when Jamal, acting as his own attorney, challenged the testimony of a prosecution witness, a cabdriver named Robert Chobert, who said, "I saw you, buddy. I saw you shoot him and I never took my eyes off you."

Jamal didn't take the stand at that trial to give his story. Nor did he call as a witness his brother, who presumably could have identified the mystery gunman. In all public statements since the trial, he has studiously avoided any discussion of the events of December 9, 1981. Reporters who get jailhouse interviews with him are told in advance they can't ask about the only moment in Jamal's life that is in any way newsworthy. All the various fantastic scenarios involving mystery gunmen come not from Jamal, but from his acolytes. What we have here is a first in history—a debate in which one of the participants holds up his end without talking.

Why the silence? On two separate occasions I asked Weinglass if he intends to stick to the mystery-gunman theory in the event Jamal wins a retrial. On both occasions he declined to comment. I upped the ante. "You're going to plead self-defense, right?" I asked. At this point he got a bit testy and called me a "prosecuting journalist."

The reason for his testiness is obvious. The search for a mystery gunman is a charade, a fund-raising stunt, a way of getting a new trial. In the event that he and his supporters outside the courtroom manage to win a retrial, Weinglass is likely to admit the obvious: that Jamal shot Faulkner. He could then claim that Jamal acted only to save his brother from a beating like that Rodney King received. (This isn't true—Cook sucker-punched Faulkner, eyewitnesses said.) He could stage a defense of the variety pioneered by Huey Newton in 1967—a political extravaganza of white guilt, inquiries into American racism, and cop-baiting. Putting the nation on trial, Weinglass might well create doubt about a few very hectic seconds of violence. The advantage to this strategy is that Weinglass doesn't have to win an acquittal. Under Pennsylvania law, any verdict below first-degree murder would permit Jamal to walk out of the courtroom the next day by virtue of time served.

This is the long-range strategy. For now, Mumia must remain silent. If he were to deny right now that he shot Faulkner, the political defense would be sidetracked because his statements could be used against him in a retrial. "You lied about shooting the officer," the prosecutor could ask. "What else are you lying about?"

Weinglass's plan may be a good one for his client, but it's an awful one for the United States. People around the world are being told that Jamal is a political prisoner who is on death row for a murder that someone else committed. It isn't true, but it's a compelling story, and he's a compelling character. On several occasions I've seen Mumia Abu-Jamal in the flesh, and he is—and this is a strange thing to say about a convicted murderer—cute. The dreadlocks, the granny glasses—he looks like a white hippie in racial drag. He reminds me not of any black person I've ever known but of my organic-farmer friend, George (who, coincidentally, is also a graduate of UCSC).

The Jamal people make a lot out of the racial nature of the case, but in fact few blacks in Philadelphia give a damn about Mumia. The MOVE group has zero popularity in the black community. The 1985 siege in which eleven MOVE members died was prompted because the neighbors of MOVE, virtually all of them black, demanded that the police do something about the noise and filth at the compound. Among the black journalists in Philadelphia, support tends to be limited to those who were friends of Jamal before the shooting. The crowds outside the courtroom are made up almost entirely of non-Philadelphians.

No, the case of Mumia Abu-Jamal does not strike a chord with most black Americans. In fact, his support comes almost exclusively from white Americans who are stuck in the sixties. These people, like the Santa Cruz students, hate the idea that actions have consequences, that a man can, in a few seconds, embark on a path that will put a permanent stain on his life. The ethos of the sixties was "If it feels good, do it." And perhaps it felt good, that night, for Mumia Abu-Jamal to take out a gun and even the score for what he perceived to be three centuries of racism. In the minds of the Jamal supporters, a balance has been struck. The racism of the Philadelphia police cancels out whatever happened the night Daniel Faulkner was shot.

In the middle of researching the Jamal case and reading his book, *Live from Death Row*, I happened to come upon a book by another black journalist/convict. The title is *Makes Me Wanna Holler*, and the author is Nathan McCall, who now writes for the *Washington Post*. McCall describes a life growing up in a solid, lower-middle-class family. In his early teens, he joined a gang. Soon he participated in the gang-rape of a scared young virgin. Then he graduated to burglaries, holdups, and gang fights; on several occasions, he shot a pistol at other teenagers who were unarmed. Eventually, his political consciousness was awakened by the Black Panthers. He drove to a suburb and walked up to the picture window of a home where a white family was watching TV. He aimed his sawed-off shotgun at the window, fired, and ran away. He never learned whether he hit anyone.

He tells these stories in a bragging tone, full of the hip slang of the black underculture. He gives the standard dissection of that underculture and shows why it was racism that caused him to commit his crimes. By the end of the book, when McCall is safely at the *Washington Post*, he clearly wants the reader to be impressed by his generosity in coming to forgive white people. He's still upset, though, by the way some white folks act. When he enters elevators alone with middle-aged white women, they shrink defensively into a corner.

This he ascribes to racism. Perhaps. But perhaps these women are just good judges of character. Perhaps they sense intuitively that they are in an extremely confined space with someone who has proven himself capable of gang-raping a child, shooting at a family, and robbing people at gunpoint. The progressive theory of criminal justice holds that the past can be eradicated. No act is irrevocable. Given enough time, evil acts stop being evil acts and become something else—material for a best-seller. Rape a child? Shoot a cop? Write a book.

The problem of Nathan McCall, and of Mumia Abu-Jamal, is the same problem Herman Melville delineated in Billy Budd—who was, however, a far more sympathetic character. Budd was by all accounts a wonderful fellow. Even the naval officers who sentenced him to death realized that he struck and killed a superior in a moment of inarticulate rage caused by that man's unfair harassment of him. Billy Budd apologized from the heart for his crime. But that didn't make the crime go away. His execution was necessary to maintain the ritual of order on a ship in wartime. "With mankind, forms, measured forms, are everything," says Captain Vere, who reluctantly orders the execution.

Melville was one of the first to be skeptical of the modern notion that human nature could be changed by the great burst of rationality that shaped the nineteenth century. You wonder what he would make of the example of novelist E. L. Doctorow. Doctorow has come to Jamal's defense not out of any understanding of the case, but out of an amorphous, damp feeling that the matter should be discussed into eternity. Doctorow wrote a piece in the *New York Times* based solely on the many distortions in Weinglass's petition for a new trial. In the piece, he refers to "Jamal's own account"—which does not exist—"that he was shot first by the officer as he approached." He concludes that a retrial should be granted.

There are several amazing things about Doctorow's piece. A man who has written extensively about crime, Doctorow didn't bother to call the Philadelphia district attorney's office and get the other side of the story. But even more amazing is that he seems to be building a theory that Jamal, having just been shot by a cop, somehow managed to get off five shots without hitting anyone while someone else came along in that same brief moment and shot the officer. Doctorow concludes, unctuously, "Will the pain of Faulkner's widow, who supports Jamal's execution, be resolved if it turns out that the wrong man has been executed and her husband's killer still walks the streets?"

If Doctorow were really concerned about "the pain of Faulkner's widow," he could simply call Maureen Faulkner and discuss it. Then he'd learn that this pain is greatly exacerbated by foolish people like him who take the side of her husband's killer without learning the facts. But few of the people who follow Mumia Abu-Jamal seem to want to think too much about the facts. They're happy with hints of a mystery gunman, and they'd like to leave it at that, floating in the air.

What they hate more than the police, more than racism, is the idea that some acts are irreversible, that a cute, reasonable-sounding guy like Mumia Abu-Jamal could have held a gun eighteen inches from the head of a man who was lying helpless on the sidewalk, pulled the trigger, and sent a hollow-point bullet into his brain, where it proceeded to expand to many times its original size. (The gun-shop owner who sold Jamal the hollow-point bullets testified at the trial as well.)

Well, tough luck, boys and girls. Jamal did it. Worse, he did it and he never once expressed any remorse, any sadness for anyone but himself. Sorry, Karla, we can't compromise. Some things are irreversible—trivial things like quotes given to a reporter and big things like a bullet in the brain. Sorry E.L., this isn't one of those Random House novels where the identity of the mystery gunman is revealed at the end. This is real life in a bad part of town. If there's a better candidate for the death penalty than a man who kills in cold blood and shows not the slightest regret, we Philadelphians haven't heard of him.

The great irony here is that if Jamal had simply told the truth at his trial and let his lawyer do his job, he probably would have been convicted of manslaughter or third-degree murder. He would have served his time by now and been released. He appears to have learned his lesson. These days, he sits quietly in court while his defense team does the talking. He is evolving. "You wait," says Maureen Faulkner. "If he ever gets a retrial, you're gonna see Jamal in a buzz haircut and a suit."

A safe bet. But it's also a safe bet Jamal will never get another trial. The rules for appeals call for the defendant to show not only that an issue was wrongly decided at trial, but also that if the decision had gone the other way, the verdict might have been reversed. In Jamal's case, that's a stiff burden. Throw out any one piece of evidence and there are still a dozen more. And the smoking gun simply won't go away.

As a radio journalist, Jamal was a failure. As a writer, he's a mediocrity. It is often said of bad writers, "He couldn't write a ransom note." That can't be said of Jamal. His entire book is a ransom note, a cleverly disguised plea to raise the ransom to get him off death row. So far it's brought in at least $800,000. But as literature, it's laughable.

In life, Mumia Abu-Jamal was little more than a sixties social experiment that failed. It's only in death that he will finally be able to do something for his fellow man. His departure, if it ever comes, will signal to all Americans—from the most august professor at the University of California to the lowliest TV star—that we human beings are irrevocably tied to our actions. It will mean that we are not condemned to frolic forever clueless among the redwoods, but that we do indeed have a civilization, and that civilization has certain rules that protect us from the whimsies of our barbaric nature.

A Death in Berkeley

I t could just as easily be 1967 instead of 1994 on this warm summer afternoon in the heart of downtown Oakland. The steps in front of the gleaming white Alameda County Courthouse are filled with young black men and women decked out in Afro wigs, berets, and black leather jackets. Clenching fists, they chant, "Free Huey! Off the Pig."

Huey, of course, is Huey Newton, who, along with Bobby Seale, founded the Black Panther Party in 1966 with a ten-point platform that included a call to armed resistance against police and who in 1967 became a radical icon while on trial for murdering an Oakland police officer. The demonstration being staged here by professional actors has the choreography of the original but not its passion. The real demonstrations that took place outside the courthouse during Newton's murder trial that summer twenty-eight years ago made him a symbol of revolutionary black manhood and launched the Black Panthers as a powerful national force that would help define the sixties.

Huey Newton died in obscurity in 1989, a crack addict killed by a young gang dealer who viewed him as a nuisance. But his legend lives on, having survived revelations that he was more a thug than a revolutionary. His name once again is magic among young blacks toying with radicalism. It pops up frequently in rap lyrics and in the casual Afrocentrisms of public education. It was on the big screen in *Panther*, the movie director Mario Van Peebles filmed in Oakland at the scene of the crime.

Meanwhile, by a serendipitous confluence of events, across the street from the set Van Peebles has created is another sign of the revival of interest in the Black Panthers. The Oakland Art Museum is co-hosting a panel discussion about the Panthers featuring Elaine Brown. Brown has become something of a legend of her own — although she, unlike Newton, is a living one. A beautiful young woman who escaped gang life in Philadelphia in the early sixties and came to California to work as a songwriter, she ended up as a dancer at Los Angeles's Pink Pussycat and as a sometime call girl (street name "Peaches") before becoming politicized and joining the Panthers. Helped by shrewd intelligence and a willingness to sleep her way to the top with Panther leaders (including, most notably, Newton himself), Brown was selected by Newton to run the organization when he fled to Cuba in 1974 to escape charges of murdering Kathleen Smith, an Oakland prostitute.

The auditorium is packed and has the feel of a reunion. In addition to Brown, familiar faces include former Panther chief of staff David Hilliard and his current partner, Frederika, Huey's widow. The Panther couple is the reigning keeper of the Huey Newton flame with their so-called Dr. Huey P. Newton Foundation, one of the sponsors of the museum's colloquy today. But Elaine Brown is the center of attention. She has been on her own comeback trail since the 1993 publication of her autobiography, A *Taste of Power*, a tale filled with hot couplings between white producers and fierce black revolutionaries and chilling tales of violent Panther crimes.

In her belated and quite partial admissions, Brown confirmed what I and many other Panther watchers have known for many years: At the heart of this organization that continues to be admired by many blacks for its message of revolutionary self-help was a criminal element, created by Newton, that practiced extortion, racketeering, and murder. Yet while it teases with hints of the truth, Brown's book is also a self-serving exoneration. That gloss-over stands in stark contrast to the astonishing revelations Brown made to me shortly after I saw her at the Oakland Museum in an exhaustive, four-hour, late-night, manic phone interview. "I was both a victim and a perpetrator of some of that shit," she told me, adopting a confessional-but-defiant attitude about the crimes of the Panthers' past. But she dropped her professional guard for the first time in a revealing moment of honest reflection in her next sentence: "I was a silent perpetrator. I'm sorry about that. My only mistakes were that I loved Huey at the time." She then reverted to form, denying any involvement in the Panther murders we had been talking about.

The victims of most of these murders were other street toughs who stood in the way of Panther attempts to muscle in on the rackets in Oakland, or else they were party members who refused to obey Newton's "revolutionary discipline." (The FBI fanned the incendiary factional disputes between the Huey Newton loyalists and Eldridge Cleaver and breakaway chapters in New York.) But one murder—that of a white bookkeeper named Betty Van Patter—was different, and it has interested me for the last twenty years. Betty, who worked for the Panthers, disappeared just before Christmas 1974 and was not seen again until January 17, 1975, when the Coast Guard fished her body out of the San Francisco Bay. Autopsy reports showed that she had been killed by a massive blow to the head. Some have traced this murder to the door of the Panthers in general and to Elaine Brown in particular. It has become not only the crime that will not die but also the crime that apparently cannot be solved.

Van Patter's unsolved murder has haunted the Bay Area Left for two decades. It was a crime covered up and surrounded with denial—a mystery that, if ever solved, could threaten the elaborate web of self-justification constructed by the Black Panthers and the white movement that unquestioningly supported the organization. After years of investigation—studying police reports and interviewing many sources close to Betty and the Panthers—I think I can finally begin to reconstruct what happened to the Panther bookkeeper.

On Friday night, December 13, 1974, Betty Van Patter grabbed her three-quarter-length camel topper, slipped her brown shoulder bag in place, and left her apartment.

Betty was still something of a looker: slender, fair-haired, and green-eyed with good cheekbones. Still, at 45, she was beginning to fray around the edges, showing the first wrinkles and the pallor of too much drinking and too many cigarettes. Normally, she would be looking forward to the relaxation offered by her favorite bar, the Berkeley Square, a place where white women could dance with black men and nobody gave a damn. But on this night she may have been feeling sad and uptight and could have been drinking because of inner turmoil.

She had been embarrassed when her twenty-four-year-old daughter, Tammy, had come over several days earlier and seen her drinking at 11:00 in the morning. She drank more white wine than she should, buying it in jug-sized quantities from the Oak Barrel, Berkeley's discount liquor emporium. But she couldn't help it. She was unhappy with the quality of her emotional relationships. She'd had little stability in her love life since splitting with her children's father, Ray Baltar, after having worked so hard with him to establish a family and a respectable life. It had been a traumatic parting. But Betty would become used to disappointments in romance.

She had met her next husband, Ken Van Patter, at an Alcoholics Anonymous meeting while recovering from the divorce, but that marriage had lasted only a few years. In the late sixties, she had next gotten involved with a young black man named Leonard Rideout who was about Tammy's age; when he went to prison for theft, she visited him faithfully. He dropped her after being paroled, although the two of them did remain friends. For the last year, she'd been seeing a near-blind black man named Ken Baptiste, who was closer to her own age and, like her, drank. Although she continued to see Ken, that affair was officially over because Betty couldn't accept his relationship with another woman.

The daytime drinking had begun only with her recent troubles at work. During the previous few months she had been excited about working for the Black Panther Party and, particularly, for Elaine Brown. She gushed to Tammy about how pretty and inspiring Brown was and wrote to her own mother, "She is a dynamic, intelligent, and forceful person, and she has given me her complete trust."

Betty was flattered when Brown befriended her and took her to Giovanni's for pizza, where the two of them buzzed like school girls with all the plans for Betty to catch up on the books for the Early Learning Center, the school the Panthers were running in East Oakland. David Horowitz, then an editor at *Ramparts*, where Betty used to work, and a board member of the school, was the one who originally suggested her for the job. He had emphasized the necessity of straightening out the messy Panther finances to keep the school legitimate, and he believed that Betty was the one for the job.

At first, she felt positive. The job provided income, but it also gave her something more: a feeling that she was participating in the movement for social justice that she, like most of the white leftists she knew in Berkeley, felt the Panthers embodied. Betty wrote to her mother of her enthusiasm in a series of letters that summer and fall. In her diary she recorded her first impressions of the Panthers' reserve toward her as a white intruder and her determination to overcome their suspicions. She was looking forward to a deepening relationship with Brown, who fostered this notion by seductively dangling the possibility that Betty could eventually work as an adviser on Brown's 1975 campaign for the Oakland City Council, a campaign that promised to be the most serious bid for political power that the Panthers had yet made.

There were strange moments. Shortly after starting work with the Panthers, Betty had written to her mother about an incident outside her house in which she ran into a man who knew her name: "I know I am being . . . watched by the Party. . . . I'm sure [the black man] is from the Party. . . . All of this intrigue isn't necessary."

But her admiration for Brown resolved all these ambiguities. After all, hadn't the Panther leader invited Betty to her lovely home in the classy Portabello Apartments on the Oakland embarcadero? Betty was so impressed with Brown's taste and fancy furniture, she told her daughter, that she decided to take out a loan from the credit union and do some redecorating of her own; in fact, she had already completed the applications.

Betty felt a little guilty spending money on herself. She had always prided herself in not taking alimony, in working to support herself and always being able to give her kids a little extra money here and there even if it meant skimping on herself. She was a soft touch who liked taking care of people. (Her daughter later said, "Although my mother was floundering [in her own life] at this time, she was a rock in all our lives.") Tammy and her brothers were used to Betty's taking in teenage Berkeley waifs and giving them sanctuary in her attic. Betty believed in giving them shelter and a nice meal and was not critical if they smoked pot or couldn't get their lives together. She liked being a refuge for her kids, for runaways, and, she admitted, for recent lovers who couldn't make a go of things.

She was making $800 a month working for the Panthers and now, after breaking up with Ken and having no more waifs at home, she thought she could spend a bit on herself. After all, Betty confided to her daughter, if Brown, a revolutionary Black Panther woman, could have a smart home with beautiful furnishings, why couldn't she?

Everything would have been fine if not for the disturbing information Betty had learned from the Panther books. After starting out as accountant for the school, she had been asked by Brown to do the accounting for the Lamp Post, the Panther bar in Oakland. The bar, with its dark, intimate interior of black walls, red-speckled black Formica tables, and gaudy chandeliers, looked like some politically correct bordello. Its walls were studded with spot-lit paintings by Panther political cartoonist Emory Douglas. The full-length portrait of Huey Newton in flat, lurid, cartoon style dominated all the other "art." Newton used the place as his own private kingdom where he hit on women, held court, and strutted his macho dominance. After Newton fled to Cuba, violent incidents continued to take place at the bar—including one killing committed by a member of the Squad, Newton's praetorian guard of gangsters who had been his gunmen when he was in Oakland and who continued to throw their weight around when he left.

Betty had jumped at the opportunity to increase her responsibilities by taking on work at the Lamp Post. Somewhat grandiosely she wrote to her mother, "It seems I am always being pressed into service to bring harmony out of chaos. It is nice to be recognized for one's own ability and that certainly seems to be mine."

Yet the view of things she got from the Lamp Post books was more than mere accounting chaos. Jimmy Ward, a cousin of Newton's, was the nominal owner of the bar, having bought it in 1970. But for all practical purposes, the Lamp Post was Panther owned and operated. It was the place where Newton laundered money gained from illicit operations in the ghetto—rackets, dope, and prostitution. (Panther attorney Fred Hiestand knew enough about the Panther bar and restaurant to gossip to David Horowitz later that a whopping $25,000 a month was coming into the Lamp Post under the table.) It was rumored that the Panthers were running hookers out of the bar and that there was dope trafficking on the premises. (The late Arlene Slaughter, the mother of Huey's second wife, Frederika Newton, told me in 1977 that she knew that Panther rank-and-file women were punished for infractions of party discipline by being put to work at the Lamp Post as hookers.)

All kinds of questionable activity took place at the bar, but while Panther higher-ups might have feared that the racketeering would come into public view, what bothered Betty most was simply that the place was not paying its taxes and risked attracting the attention of the IRS. The register tapes wouldn't lie; and she, as the bookkeeper, couldn't—and wouldn't—cover it up. She complained obliquely to her daughter, Tammy. She also complained to Leonard Rideout, her former boyfriend, whom she'd seen only a few days earlier. She wanted to tell him everything that was going on with the Panther books but couldn't trust him quite that far. She did tell him that she was going to have a summary meeting with Brown to discuss what was troubling her and hinted that she knew secrets that would give her leverage in the meeting. Rideout didn't take her seriously. He thought she was just trying to seem important with her talk.

Back in November, Betty had also called Lillian Weil, a certified public accountant. Weil once did the books for the irrigation company founded by Betty's first husband, Ray Baltar, and had, in fact, taught Betty bookkeeping. Betty asked Weil if she would work as an outside consultant to help square the Lamp Post accounts.

Weil was wary of the Panthers. ("I had a client, a plumbing contractor, down on East 14th," she says. "The Black Panthers went up and down East 14th demanding funds in threatening word and manner. It was a shakedown.") She had warned Betty about them, but she respected her decision to ignore the warning. The morning of December 13, in fact, Betty picked up the flow charts Lillian had prepared for the Lamp Post, which Betty felt would clear up the income and outgo and prevent people from raiding the bar's till.

From all accounts, Betty's next stop was a meeting with Brown to talk about her plans for straightening out the books. It was an appointment she had sought repeatedly but that Brown agreed to only after Betty made threats about quitting and perhaps going public. (Brown was later taped as saying, "She called me and left this message — 'Elaine's gonna describe my role to me or I'm leaving. . . .' She said, 'I'll leave this whole fucking operation, do you want me to do that?' These were her words, the last thing she said to me.") With her accountant's optimism, Betty still believed the problem was simply one of figures and could be fixed. But Brown, of course, knew that the figures were only the tip of the iceberg. Their meeting degenerated. Brown later said, "She accused me of trying to be some kind of queen" — and after a wild argument Brown fired her.

When Betty left her apartment on Haste Street later that day, she drove the short distance to the Berkeley Square on University Avenue. She went in, greeted several acquaintances at the bar, and perched on a stool away from the fireplace. She had a drink by herself at the bar. Regulars at the Square noted that she appeared particularly depressed. But she didn't confide in them that she had been fired; instead she mentioned that she expected her onetime lover Ken Baptiste to meet her there later.

Not long after she arrived, several patrons recalled later, a tall black man came into the Square and gave Betty a note. Then he left. Almost immediately, she followed him out. That was the last time anyone but her murderers saw Betty Van Patter alive.

Tammy couldn't reach her mother over that weekend and decided to go to her apartment on Monday. She was greeted there by her brother Greg, who had arrived unexpectedly from Sacramento late Friday. His mother and her car were both gone. But when he woke on Saturday morning, his mother was still absent, although her car was inexplicably parked in its assigned slot at the apartment building. When Tammy heard this, her worry turned to panic. Her mother was no walker and never went anywhere without her car. Furthermore, Betty had made no arrangements to feed her cat.

On Tuesday, Tammy called Ken Baptiste, her mother's ex-boyfriend, who called Betty's work number with the Panthers. He reported, "Somebody told me your mother doesn't work there anymore." Incredulous, Tammy called the office herself. A woman who identified herself as Ruby said Betty didn't work there any longer but refused to provide details and hung up on her. Tammy called David Horowitz, whom she'd met a few times when visiting her mother at *Ramparts*. "My mother's missing," she blurted out. Horowitz responded, "Oh, my God!" and told her he would make some calls and get back to her. When he called Tammy back, she detected fear in his voice. He said that he had just talked to Elaine Brown, who'd told him she'd fired Betty. "Go to the police!" Horowitz told Tammy. "Go to the police!"

Horowitz had reason to worry. Two months earlier, a Panther had been shot and killed at a dance at the Panther school. Betty knew about the killing and seemed to accept Brown's explanation that the Panther had been "set up." But as a result of the incident Horowitz had decided to avoid the Panther school (soon he would quit the board and sever all connections with the organization). Another problem for him was the entourage Elaine had assembled. "Suddenly I noticed the people around Elaine weren't so benign," Horowitz says. "These guys looked mean." Indeed, Brown was anything but a moderating influence on the party. As her book candidly indicates, she saw the task of acquiring authority in a macho, violent organization as a challenge. Not long after Betty Van Patter's body was discovered floating in San Francisco Bay, Brown presided over the disciplining of a Panther by her security force. While a shotgun was pointed at the victim, four Panthers stomped him to the floor. At the conclusion of the brutal beating, she writes, "the floor was rumbling, as though a platoon of pneumatic drills were breaking through its foundation. Blood was everywhere. [His] face disappeared."

Feeling paranoid and personally vulnerable, Horowitz had secretly taped his two phone calls to Brown about Betty, although he didn't tell Tammy about this at the time of their conversation. The tapes reveal a vicious and vulgar attitude toward Betty by Brown. Worse, they show a callous disregard for the disappearance of a former employee and for the agony of her family. "I'm saying if her daughter hasn't seen her, she should have told her daughter she didn't work for us anymore. . . . She made me so mad it's hard for me even to be concerned about her daughter. . . . She was just stupid. . . . She was just an idiot and she annoyed me. . . . I mean this woman has all our little information and shit. . . ."

When Horowitz pressed her further about whether she knew anything about Betty, Brown said with irritation, "I don't know where she is. Why call me like I'm some kind of a criminal? . . . I fired her." When Horowitz pressed her further, Brown snapped, "She disappeared last Friday. She didn't work for us before last Friday. . . . I'm saying she lost this job before." Brown was concerned only with the negative implications Betty's disappearance could have on her campaign and declared her intention to "call [Panther criminal attorney Charles] Garry, just in case the daughter acts too crazy."

The conversations convinced Horowitz that the Panthers were involved in Betty's disappearance. In their talk, Brown had unwittingly supplied a possible motive: "Let me tell you something about Betty. Betty wanted to know too much of everything. . . . She started telling me about why [the Lamp Post] taxes need to be paid. . . . She started asking me so many questions about stuff that was not her business. . . . She says, 'Well I want to know what you're going to do with your [City Council] campaign.' . . . She's asking too many questions. . . ." Clearly, Brown was worried that Betty would go public.

Because she didn't know about the content of these conversations, Tammy Baltar at first ignored Horowitz's urgings that she go to the police. "He didn't explain why or anything," she says today in a voice that still tightens with remembered fear. "I'm just this twenty-four-year-old kid, not really coping with any of this very well. My mother's status at that point gave me reason to believe she just might have gone off somewhere to be by herself if something traumatic had happened."

Besides, in the radical culture of that era, the police were not to be trusted. This was especially true when it came to the Panthers, who had successfully perpetuated the myth that the police were engaging in a "genocidal campaign" against them. So, instead of taking Horowitz's advice, Baltar called Paul Jacobs, left-wing journalist and social critic who had cultivated the role of the conscience of the radical community. Jacobs, in turn, referred her to Bay Area private investigator Harold Lipsett.

Hal Lipsett had made himself into a local legend for such antics as creating the "bugged" olive, which could be placed in a martini so that intimate conversations could be overheard. (He was one of the inspirations for Francis Ford Coppola's private eye in *The Conversation*.) He worked the glitzy Nob Hill divorce cases, but he had also developed something of a subspecialty working for left-wing attorneys like Charles Garry (now dead) on cases involving Huey Newton and other Panthers. Nobody was better connected than Lipsett.

After Tammy talked to him, Lipsett made brief inquiries. She took notes when he made his initial report to her: "The [Panther] headquarters are hot. They know she's missing. You should go to the police now. Leave your office. Go over to Berkeley to the police department and report her missing. Now!"

Finally convinced, Tammy put down the receiver, hopped on a BART train, and went to the police station. It had been more than a week since her mother's disappearance. "I think there's something you should know about my mother," Tammy remembers telling a Berkeley detective as she filed her report. "She's the bookkeeper for the Black Panther Party." The detective immediately rose and left the room. When he returned, it was with Detective Michael O'Keefe, the de facto supervisor of such cases. O'Keefe's involvement elevated the case above that of the average missing person report.

During the next week, the Berkeley police did all the routine leg-work of checking motels and taxi records, interviewing acquaintances and friends. Tammy let police into her mother's house to try to deter-mine when she was last there. (One clue: Betty's birth control pills had been punched through Thursday, December 12.) There were interviews with Black Panthers too, and investigators noted in their reports that the Panthers were not forthcoming with details. One offi-cer wrote the following about Joan Kelley, who headed the Panther school: "Kelley was very evasive when questioned about the nature and scope of the victim's employment and the circumstances of her hiring and termination. She would not confirm the date of hiring or of termination, nor provide the specific reason for termination."

More revealing was the investigator's call to Ken Baptiste, Betty's erstwhile boyfriend, who was to meet her at the Berkeley Square the night of her disappearance. Baptiste said that Betty had told him in their last conversation that she had obtained an appointment to see Elaine Brown "regarding her job." He told police that he had stopped by the Berkeley Square to meet Betty, but that regulars at the bar told him she'd just left. Baptiste told police that he had, in fact, made a concerted effort to find Betty that night—first phoning

her home and then calling some of their other watering holes at the
Marriott Hotel bar and Solomon Grundy's restaurant on the Berkeley waterfront. More important, he'd also called the Lamp Post. The
police reported Baptiste's account of that phone call in these words:
"At the Lamp Post, a male answered the telephone. Baptiste asked
that the victim be paged and was put on hold. A woman came back
on the line and said, 'That party has left.' Baptiste drew the conclusion that she had been there that very Friday night prior to his call."

It wasn't until January 23, six days after Van Patter's corpse was
recovered and after repeated requests from the police to Panther
attorney Fred Hiestand, that Elaine Brown finally agreed to meet
with Berkeley cops. (An autopsy showed that Betty's body had been
in the water fewer than half of the thirty-six days she had been
missing, which led her children to fear that she had been held under
terrifying circumstances while her fate was debated.) They
convened in the San Francisco office of the Panthers' long-time
criminal defense attorney, Charles Garry. Complaining that she was
being blemished with this accusation as a way of harming her City
Council campaign, Brown told police she'd had contact with Betty
only three or so times in her life. Brown snidely noted that Betty was
a flake who had not come to work on one occasion because of an
adverse astrological forecast. She further characterized Betty as a
whiner who continually complained about her job, "insufficient
working space," and her black office assistant. Betty was "high strung
and getting on people's nerves."

Elaine had already put out the word through the Panther civil
attorney, Fred Hiestand, a white lawyer formerly with Public Advo-
cates, that Betty had been fired on December 6, a full week before
she disappeared. During the police interview, she angrily waved
Betty's severance check, dated the sixth, as if the cops were too stupid to figure out that any check can be backdated. (The check,
moreover, had not been cashed.)

In any case, others contradicted Brown's claim that Betty had
been fired a week before her disappearance. A later police report

of an interview with Lillian Weil stated, "Weil said that at that time the victim seemed to be very enthusiastic about her work and behaved in a manner totally inconsistent with having been fired a week prior, as is alleged by Elaine Brown. . . . Weil said that Van Patter also told her that the Lamp Post account was made difficult by the practice of payroll kickbacks and of excessive cash expenditures."

Fred Hiestand, Brown's own adviser, told police he had seen Betty on December 10, three days before her disappearance, when he discussed other Panther matters with her. He also told police she had seemed "enthusiastic" about her job. In point of fact, as the taped conversation between Brown and David Horowitz shows, Betty had used the occasion of the meeting with Hiestand to seek a sympathetic ear in which to lodge her complaints about irregularities at the Lamp Post. ("Betty calls me and starts threatening me with 'Look, either you gonna. . . . Do you want me to quit? . . .' and then she goes to Hiestand and tells Hiestand that she thinks what we're doing is shaky at the Lamp Post.") Obviously, Hiestand had reported the contents of the conversation to Elaine Brown, whereupon Elaine had become outraged that the bookkeeper was meddling in things that didn't concern her.

Tammy Baltar had her own reasons to doubt Brown's story. Her mother had made plans several days after the alleged firing to give her a tour of her office. "Why would Mom invite me to her office if she'd been fired?" she wondered. Moreover, Tammy knew her mother had refinanced a credit loan on Thursday, the day before her disappearance, to fix up her apartment. She wouldn't have done this had she lost her job days earlier.

In her police interview in Garry's office, Brown also lied outright when she told police there was no connection between the Lamp Post and the Panther Party. (Later on, in A Taste of Power, she would be more truthful: "The Lamp Post was a complete Black Panther Party operation.") In fact, in the conversations Horowitz taped, Brown made it clear that she was responsible for expanding Betty's duties to include the Lamp Post books.

But none of these contradictions were ever explored. Charles Garry abruptly cut off the January 23 interview between Brown and the Berkeley police. Authorities never again interviewed Brown on the Van Patter homicide. Although they would never admit it, Berkeley police, while they had strong suspicions in the case, were intimidated by all the charges of police brutality and harassment leveled at them by radicals over the years.

Lillian Weil, who believes the Panthers murdered Betty, feels that this was the case. She recalls a conversation with Detective Michael O'Keefe in which he told her, "Well, you know we just can't go after them." O'Keefe was more specific with Peter Collier. When Collier, who had also known Betty at *Ramparts*, called to plead with him to pursue the Panther connection, O'Keefe replied that it was ironic that white radicals who had spent years emasculating the police in cases involving the Panthers would now urge them on when one of their own was the victim.

The suspicions of Weil, Collier, and others that the police were cowed by the Panthers' political muscle and fearful of once again being made to look like "pigs" in the investigation seemed borne out by the abrupt resignation of O'Keefe from the police force. In 1975, he sent Tammy Baltar a private message in which he expressed his sense of "futility" and his sadness that he could not do more for her on the case, leading Tammy to believe that her mother's unsolved murder was perhaps a contributing factor in his decision to leave law enforcement. (O'Keefe today insists the Van Patter case languished because of jurisdictional conflict between San Mateo, where the corpse was found, and Berkeley, where the missing persons report was first filed, and denies this case triggered his resignation.) Whatever the explanation for the curious circumspection of the Berkeley Police Department, the investigation was eventually deemed inactive with no clear suspects.

Betty Van Patter's murder became one of those unsolved cases that are whispered about in a sort of code by those who doubt the official version. A handful of people had suspicions about what happened to the Panthers' bookkeeper but kept their ideas to themselves for fear of what might happen to them. (In one of their taped conversations, Brown had lightly warned David Horowitz to be careful because she didn't want him to suffer an "accident" that could be attributed to her.) In Berkeley, a radical double standard held that whatever Huey Newton and his organization did was justified by the historical sufferings of black people.

I first wrote about the underside of the Panthers in *New Times* in 1978, when I was still a member in good standing of the radical community. Peter Collier and David Horowitz mentioned Betty Van Patter's death and their suspicions of Panther involvement in their book *Destructive Generation*. Horowitz, in particular, attempted to maintain a drumbeat of remembrance on behalf of Betty. He retained an obsessive interest in uncovering the reality behind the Panthers. Over the years, he spoke with disaffected former party members and pieced together a picture of the organization that suggested there had been, almost from the beginning, two Black Panther parties. On the surface were the low-level Panther cadres who believed in the school, the Breakfast for Children program, and the other reformist aspects of the Panther program. But at a deeper stratum was the sinister element of criminals known as the Squad, a sort of armed guard with which Newton had surrounded himself in his increasingly demented, cocaine-fueled drive to control the rackets in Oakland. This view is borne out by my own research. Members of the Squad were hand-picked for their street toughness and sealed off from the rank and file engaged in the legitimate programs that gave the party its protective coloration. The Squad kept out of sight when Newton blandished the white radicals who supported the Panthers for political reasons. After dark, his bullies accompanied him in his voyages into the netherworld of Oakland's ghetto, where he assumed the role of a violent black Scarface.

The memory of this unsolved murder might have faded away altogether if not for the publicity attending *A Taste of Power*. Brown's book contained such false claims and gratuitous nastiness against her mother that Tammy Baltar, whose politics remained leftish in all the intervening years, finally told me what she'd hesitated to say to others before: "I had to admit to myself the Panthers killed my mother."

Tammy came to her conclusions as a direct result of the investigation she and her brothers commissioned detective Hal Lipsett to undertake in 1983, nearly a decade after the murder. Lipsett had simply made a few calls in 1975 when Tammy first contacted him. But in 1983, the family had enough money to pay him for a full investigation. Tammy quotes Lipsett as telling her, after he had worked on the case for months, "You should have no doubt that your mother's death was Panther related. They did it." Lipsett also warned that if she were too public in her accusations, he could not guarantee her safety. (Huey Newton was still alive at this point.)

Tammy didn't know how to act on Lipsett's information. And so, once again, she resigned herself to living with her doubts and fears. But with the publication of Brown's autobiography a decade later, Baltar sought out Lipsett again and asked him to review with her the specifics of the case. She has not revealed this information until now.

Retrieving a file in his San Francisco office on April 7, 1993, the famous detective produced one document in his own handwriting. Balter says, "He flipped to this little message paper. . . . It said: 'Elaine ordered it.' The second line had just Flores Forbes' name. The last line said 'talk with Otis,' meaning Sheldon Otis, Newton's first attorney when he came back to stand charges from Cuba."

Lipsett's information came at the end of a line of inquiry fitfully pursued by others over the years. For some, the logical suspect in Betty's death was Squad member Robert Heard, Newton's 6-foot, 7-inch, 400-pound "bodyguard" who had been the trigger man on other murders. But, according to Fred Hiestand, Elaine found Flores Forbes, another member of the Squad, to be "more manageable than Bob Heard." In addition to being what Hiestand calls "her driver," Forbes was always with her, just as Heard had always been Huey's shadow. Private investigator David Feccheimer, who worked on Panther cases as an aide to Hal Lipsett, reports that Forbes was present whenever he met with Elaine. (In 1977, Forbes, who already had a long rap sheet, was involved in an attempt by members of the Squad to assassinate a witness who was able to testify that Newton had killed Kathleen Smith, the Oakland prostitute. In the confusion of the ensuing gun battle, Forbes killed fellow Panther Louis Johnson and was later convicted of second-degree murder.)

In April 1981, while awaiting trial in Boston for a murder unrelated to Betty's, Heard sent a handwritten note to Alameda County assistant district attorney Tom Orloff offering to cut a deal in exchange for telling what he knew about "the death of the accountant that was doing the Panther books." He also warned, "If the contents of this letter leaks out, then my family will be murdered."

Orloff flew to see Heard in May, but by the time he got there, Heard had already pleaded guilty to reduced charges in the Boston matter (he served four years for manslaughter) and was no longer interested in talking about Betty Van Patter.

Heard also toyed briefly with me when he was in prison. I telephoned him to ask if he would talk to me for my book on Huey Newton. Heard asked if there might be money in exchange for telling what he knew. When no money was forthcoming, Heard withdrew cooperation. "It would be bad for black people," he said, "and besides, the statute of limitations never runs out on murder."

"It was pretty obvious," says Orloff, who has recently been elected district attorney of Alameda County, "that there was Panther involvement in the murder. First of all was the motive: Betty had been making all those complaints, looking like she might go public; second, . . . the contradictory statements Elaine gave; and third . . . a lack of any other suspects. But it's a big leap from that to making a case. Certain of her remarks [on the Horowitz tapes] might have strengthened the motive in Elaine's case, but that doesn't necessarily mean she did it."

Even if she did order the killing, Orloff adds, "It's unlikely any witnesses would come forward. It's like Mafia hits: there's a conspiracy of silence."

David Horowitz had developed his own theory about the murder after talking with Newton in 1982. Recognizing that Horowitz had been an effective fund-raiser for the Panther School, Newton tried to placate him by engaging him in a long and intimate conversation. It soon became clear, however, that the purpose of the meeting was to allow Newton to accuse Elaine Brown, whom he had "expelled" from the party upon returning from his Cuban exile, of Betty Van Patter's murder. Newton seemed to protest too much. Horowitz realized with the force of an epiphany that Newton was lying and that it was he, Newton, the head of the party even while in exile, who had given the go-ahead on the hit and that Brown had obediently carried out his orders.

It was certainly true that when Newton did return from Cuba, Brown was soon on her way out—the perfect scapegoat. Perhaps she had expected Huey never to leave Cuba, although she never stopped working for his return. Perhaps she felt that by acting as an agent of his will she would be secure in her leadership position if and when he did return. Perhaps she fantasized that she would have him back as her lover and that she would rule alongside him as Queen of the Panthers. Having witnessed Newton's unpredictable and murderous side, she should have known better. Some claim that Elaine was badly beaten before she disappeared from Oakland in 1978. Brown says, however, that she left upon seeing members of the Squad beat up her good friend and Panther colleague, Phyliss Jackson. She herself suddenly fled in the middle of the night, like so many others, submitting a formal letter of resignation months later. After laying low for months following her escape, Brown surfaced in Los Angeles and then got a job with Motown Records. Eventually she moved to France and met a wealthy white French industrialist, a tile manufacturer who has taken care of her ever since. She stayed underground for years and did not reemerge in Panther circles until she attended Newton's funeral in 1989.

Private eye David Feccheimer recently told me of a conversation he had with Panther attorney Charles Garry and Garry's assistant Pat

Richards. "They told me the Panthers committed the murder," Feccheimer said. He denied that he learned who carried out the orders and says, "I didn't want to know." But when Lipsett showed Tammy Baltar the cryptic note containing the four points he had learned about the murder, including Flores Forbes' name, Feccheimer's initials and the date of the conversation between the two detectives was on the upper corner of the paper.

In the spring of 1993, as Elaine Brown toured the country touting her autobiography, Big Bob Heard was seen in the Boston audience and Flores Forbes accompanied her to the West Coast. She denies being friendly with Heard and insists that Forbes, who did five years for his second-degree murder conviction, was her bodyguard. She calls him "a decent man and no gunslinger." In fact, Forbes is now a trained city planner with his own film company—Hod Carrier Productions.

The question of who was really running the Panther party while Newton was in Cuba—that is, who would have given the orders to eliminate a perceived enemy like Van Patter—came up again when Brown appeared at Cody's bookstore in Berkeley.

Escorted by an admiring Flores Forbes, who positioned himself along the wall in a protective stance reminiscent of the Secret Service, Brown was still stunningly beautiful and a compelling, witty speaker. Dressed for success in a pinstripe business suit and dripping with diamonds, she spoke to a standing-room-only crowd. (She had just appeared at a colloquy for Random House in New York hosted by PBS's Charlayne Hunter-Gault. There, Brown had described her politics today as "communist with a small c," to which fellow panelist Stanley Crouch—no doubt in reaction to Brown's diamond-studded chic—quipped, "and getting smaller all the time!")

In her talk at the bookstore, Brown presented herself as the harried and triumphant Panther leader, alone at the helm of a besieged organization met with hard times, a woman making it in the most manly of men's worlds. But over the years, Panther watchers (myself included) had heard from many sources and seen examples of Huey Newton's continued firm hand guiding the Panther affairs from Cuba through close advisers and friends such as Hollywood producer Bert Schneider or attorney Fred Hiestand. During the question period at Cody's, I asked Brown if she had been in touch with Newton when he was in Cuba. When she hesitated, I asked her about an anecdote in her book in which she tells of smuggling, among other items, $10,000 in cash in her underpants to Newton in Cuba.

"That must have been quite a wad," I said.

"It was," Brown laughed along with the audience.

"How did that come about? How did you know what to bring?"

Then Brown admitted that she was, indeed, in close touch with Newton. "Quite a bit, in fact," she said. "And I have the phone bills to prove it because he would call collect. It was costing me three and four thousand dollars a month!" But then she went on to insist that they hadn't talked politics. Their talks had been merely the billing and cooing of two lovers, even though Newton was at that point married to his long-time secretary, Gwen Fontaine, who loved him deeply and had accompanied him into exile.

It was clear from Brown's appearance that the woman who probably passed orders for Betty Van Patter's slaying not only got away with it but was also thriving. She was the Teflon Panther. Her book, along with David Hilliard's, has been purchased by movie producer Paula Weinstein (The Way We Were) for yet another Panther film. She has taken the first steps toward a political rehabilitation that now includes starting a Panther-type school in Oakland for inner-city youths. Even her own literary revelations of her participation in vicious beatings, extortion rip-offs, and thievery from federal and local grants—even her apparent tolerance of unchecked violence by the Squad, her offering to mop up the blood of Newton's innocent victims, her own slapping around of a white woman attorney she hated because she'd involved herself with black men—had done little to alter her image in the media as a smart and savvy survivor.

In our lengthy conversation that night after her Oakland Museum appearance, I found in Brown much of the old spellbinder who had come close to being elected to the Oakland City Council and who had gone to the 1976 Democratic convention as a Jerry Brown delegate. She did a convincing nightclub imitation of someone chastened by the experiences she'd gone through as a Panther — sadder but wiser, bloodied but unbowed. She was by turns contrite and tearfully self-exculpating. But the old knife's edge so many had feared in the seventies entered her voice again when I raised the subject of Panther murders that occurred on her watch, especially the murder of Betty Van Patter: "I knew the woman, and she's not the little nice white lady. She was into some weird shit. . . . I did everything possible for the bitch, and then I fired her."

Brown's position remains that the murder of the bookkeeper was a footnote to the history of the Panthers. Brown says she stands by the ends of the Black Panther Party and its "social mission."

Tammy Baltar and her brothers were so rankled by Elaine Brown's triumphal book tour and self-reinvention that they (accompanied by Hal Lipsett) met with law enforcement officials to see if there was any chance of reopening the investigation into their mother's death. They were also disgusted by Brown's gratuitously nasty and false charge in A *Taste of Power* that Betty had done time for drug use. As a result of their complaints, the publisher deleted the passage from the book's paperback edition. But that was the extent of their victories. A sadder but wiser Tom Orloff, who had been defeated so often by the Panthers and their attorneys and the white radical community that claimed that any prosecution was a government plot, knew that without a confession from someone involved in the murder there would be no chance of a conviction. He turned Tammy Baltar's request down.

And so, twenty years later, Betty Van Patter's unquiet ghost continues to haunt all those involved — a testament about the times and a reproach to those who didn't want to hear the bad news.

Writing About Black Panthers and Black People

T he scene is a bookstore at the corner of 6th Avenue and 22nd Street in New York City. The time is 7:20 P.M. I'm about to give a reading from my new book, *The Shadow of the Panther: Huey Newton and the Price of Black Power in America*. About thirty seats have been set up. By the time I start, all of them are filled. Most of the people in attendance are white and female, but in the first row in the right-hand corner, a black man dressed in Afrocentric clothing is sitting with his arms crossed and resting on his chest. As I walk to the podium I nod to him and to the rest of the audience. Unlike everyone else, he stares at me with belligerence. Obviously, he is trying to intimidate me. I decide that it won't work. I also decide that he is probably an ex–Black Panther come to do his best to tear me apart.

As the reading proceeds, more people show up. Barnes and Noble staffers add more chairs. But soon there are not enough chairs to go around, and latecomers have to stand. Most of the latecomers are black, confirming an old joke told in the black community: There's standard time, and there's "colored people" time. The new arrivals cluster in the background. This brings the turnout, I'm later told by someone on the Barnes and Noble staff, to approximately eighty people. I read passages from the book. The first one tells of Huey Newton's actual murder. Next, I read a passage that takes readers back to the most harrowing period of the civil rights movement, the early 1960s. The passage is about a guy named Joe Blum and how he came to the movement; it is designed to demonstrate that a disproportionately high percentage of nonblacks involved in the movement were young Jews. But first I tell the audience of my dissatisfaction with Michael Kazin, a left-wing academic who reviewed my book and took me to task for not taking a more empirical approach to such a controversial subject as the Black Panther Party. In the book I admit that *The Shadow of the Panther* is not meant to be a comprehensive history of the entire party. It is designed to tell of how the stage was set to establish the party's legitimacy, when and how it was founded, what happened to select rank-and-file members within the party, how the Panthers turned into a gang of thugs, and what happened to the founder of the party that led to his death early one morning in August 1989.

So, I ask the audience rhetorically, why am I being taken to task for not doing what this academic, one of those nostalgia artists who call themselves sixties historians, wishes I had done? I'll leave it to people like him to write the kind of book he suggests. (In a desperate attempt to discredit my book, young Kazin also took me to task for being off a page number or two in books I cited in fifty-two pages of footnotes!)

And then the question-and-answer period begins. The first question comes from the belligerent-looking man who has been sitting in the front row. And, as happened at a forum on my book at my alma mater, Brown University, this first comment is not a question. It is a minispeech given by a survivor of the era. He tells everyone that he is a Black Panther veteran who was an officer in one of the East Coast branches. His minispeech ignores the fact that during the course of my reading (at which he has been present from beginning to end), I stated that my book is about the West Coast Panthers. He makes it clear that it doesn't matter that I described the major rift that developed between the East Coast branches and the Oakland headquarters over the West Coast's mismanagement of money and the fascist tactics used by West Coast Panthers left in charge of the party while Huey Newton was in jail from 1967 to 1970 (tactics that eventually would pale next to those used by Huey himself after he emerged from prison). Neither does it matter to him that I made it quite clear there were well-meaning members of the party who tried to do good for the black community. He is angry because I mentioned anything negative at all in the party and did not contact him for his take on the era.

This man's attitude demonstrates why it is so difficult to write an objective history of almost any aspect of life in black America. An anti-intellectual attitude is rampant in the black community. Underlying this attitude is a belief that stepping back and looking at all aspects of black America—the bad as well as the good—is treasonous. The people holding this attitude truly believe that the worst blight on human history is what white America did to blacks. Most of them haven't read a single book of history that would indicate, for instance, that Jews and a variety of white ethnic groups have also suffered atrocities at the hands of others, atrocities every bit as horrible as, and in some cases worse than, what black Americans have suffered. These narrow-minded arbiters of black history promote romantic visions of black Africa, ignoring the history of interethnic rivalries that caused most of the slaves taken from the continent to be captured and sold to Europeans by other black Africans. They blame what's happening in Rwanda in the 1990s on colonial history, as though Hutus are so mindless that they cannot themselves be held accountable for brazenly pulling the trigger on and applying machetes to Tutsis. "The legacy left by the French made them do it," state black romantics who insist on turning all of black history into fairy tales of glorious kings and queens who lived blissful lives until the white man arrived on their territory.

The roundabout manner in which such attitudes insult the intelligence of all black people is lost on those like my questioner. Before

I can interrupt the man and tell him to save his speech for and if and when he writes his own book, he calls me a traitor to black people. He implies that my fate will be the same as that of all other "traitors" who accuse the Black Panthers of having been thugs. I am amazed how it is lost on him and his late-arriving supporters gathered in the back (who egg him on) that they are dramatizing everything about the party that I criticized in my reading and make clear in my book—especially its intolerance of dissent. I am amazed that he is demonstrating the very reason that black America has the problems it has: Dissenters are dealt with by being silenced.

But I realize that this man is really no different from some of the people I interviewed for my book. In *The Shadow of the Panther*, for instance, party veteran Landon Williams comes out looking very good. I describe him as someone who once genuinely believed in violent revolution. I distinguish between him and those in the party—most of the Panthers—who were merely thugs looking for an excuse to pick up a gun and engage in mayhem. I tell readers how Williams left the party, disgusted by the behavior of Huey Newton and others who turned to outright criminal brutality. At the end of my book I also talk about Williams's afterlife as a neighborhood development planner. Despite all of this, Williams is so dissatisfied with my book's conclusions that he has denounced it wherever he goes.

I called him in June after sending him five complimentary copies of the book. During the call Williams theorized about why I wrote the book and who put me up to it. "You were hired by the right wing to put a black face on what they've been saying about us all along. You took advantage of us for your own selfish gain."

I reminded him that I had explained to him what I wanted to do three years before the book was published. The only difference was that as my research progressed, my opinion of the party had changed because I had come to see the extent to which earlier ideals had been a cover for criminal intention among Newton and his comrades. Williams then gave a telling response: "If your opinion of the party was changing, then you should have called me and gotten my permission to still use everything I told you."

The totalitarian implications of such a way of thinking—part and parcel of what the Black Panther Party was all about—appear to be lost today, decades after the fact, on someone like Williams, who has otherwise been at pains to distance himself from some of the insanity of the party. Given such an attitude, can there be any question of why the Black Panther Party was doomed to self-destruct?

When I began researching *The Shadow of the Panther* I was convinced that the Black Panthers were heroes. My initial interest in the subject dates back to childhood and the fact that my birth name is Huey. I wasn't named after Newton, as the editor at Addison-Wesley responsible for getting me to write the book initially thought. I was named after my father ten years before Huey Newton became a god of the Left. Actually, I always hated the name Huey, and for many years I felt an undercurrent of anger and resentment toward my father, who was a physician, both for giving me a name I was constantly teased about (other children compared me to the cartoon duck, Baby Huey) and for raising me and my two sisters in a black neighborhood where the other kids resented us because their fathers worked in factories. The kids, encouraged by their parents, were convinced we thought we were better than they. It was all part of the built-in nihilism that keeps so many black people from achieving anything constructive. Such thinking holds that those black people who achieve something out of the ordinary have separated themselves from other blacks and allowed themselves to become "less black."

The black power/Black Panther era of the late 1960s reinforced these ideas and taught that true blacks—"the brothers on the block"—are those at the bottom. Those who are not at the bottom or who don't use their talents to take care of those at the bottom are trying to act white or bourgeois. Such sixties thinking holds that individualism is wrong, capitalist rather than socialist by its very nature. It teaches that blacks have been wronged and that atonement for the wrongs committed against blacks can only be collective in nature. (A distinction must be drawn between the cultural nationalists of the era who taught outright hatred of whites and the Black Panthers, who didn't teach hatred of whites but taught hatred of capitalism and those whites who upheld it.)

Such "pro-masses" thinking seemed very chic back in the sixties and, for some, still does. But it is rooted not only in trendy Marxism, but also in the way the slaves were taught to accept their lot. Any slave who didn't accept it was a danger to the system. And even though many slaves were not convinced of their inferiority, most were conditioned to always feel connected to even the worst-off slave. Thus any gain achieved that raised one person's lot even a little bit was shared with the rest. Hold on to nothing (was the motto), including any individual ambitions. And one final aspect of this mind-set endemic to so much of black America has to do with excusing failure. Any black who advances gives the lie to the notion that blacks can't improve themselves because they are the victims of a racist society. Achievers must be summarily dealt with, brought back to the bottom with the rest of the blacks, where all "belong."

While growing up in Fort Wayne, Indiana, I experienced all these aspects of a mind-set that works to keep African Americans in a kind of bondage. I myself bought into it for a while, feeling somewhat guilty and "less black" because my father had raised himself up to the position of a professional. In 1968, Huey Newton was the first Huey I was exposed to who was looked up to by masses of blacks at the bottom. So at the age of eleven I read everything about him and his Black Panther Party for Self-Defense that I could get my hands on. My reading of the situation, beginning in 1966 when black power was first advanced philosophically by members of the Student Nonviolent Coordinating Committee (SNCC), taught me that doing my schoolwork was acting white. So I got bad grades from the third to the sixth grade. The first thing that saved me from permanent scholastic failure was the potential embarrassment of entering junior high school the following year at the bottom of the tracking system.

But even as my grades improved, I kept my fantasies about Huey Newton and the Black Panthers—at least until 1973, when they began to fade out of the national limelight. I forgot all about the party until August 1989. In the intervening years I achieved academic success at my predominantly white high school, thanks largely to David Halberstam's book *The Best and the Brightest*. The book, which was about how the United States became involved in Vietnam, absorbed me primarily because most of the key characters, except for Lyndon Johnson, attended elite universities. Halberstam's stress on the personalities involved in the making of history convinced me that in order to achieve, a person needed to go to such a school. I set my sights on Brown University, which I attended from 1975 to 1979, graduating with a bachelor's degree in biomedical ethics.

I attended medical school at my father's alma mater—predominantly black Meharry Medical College in Nashville, Tennessee. I grew less and less interested in my medical studies. In 1982 I dropped out and began graduate school in urban planning at the New School for Social Research in New York City. Then I became a project manager at the Harlem Urban Development Corporation (HUDC). In May 1986 I quit HUDC out of frustration with its bureaucracy and set out to become a writer. Over a two-year period, I worked a variety of odd jobs to make ends meet—taxi driver, paralegal, messenger, and the like. By May 1988 I saw my first story published in a major newspaper: an opinion editorial in *New York Newsday*. The following year I began shopping my *Newsday* clips to newspapers nationally, in search of a full-time position as an editorial writer.

Then in August 1989, I received a letter from Robert C. Maynard, publisher of the *Oakland Tribune*, inviting me to join his staff when he could open the appropriate position. That same month Huey Newton was shot and killed. It shocked me to learn that Newton's death was drug-related. In November, with nothing more than

Maynard's invitation (which never materialized into a definite job offer, due to the *Tribune's* poor financial health), I headed west. I was determined to secure a full-time writing position in the San Francisco Bay Area and to find out what led to my childhood hero's ignoble end.

Within months of moving to San Francisco, I became an associate editor at San Francisco–based Pacific News Service. The Newton story continued to fascinate me, and I began to research a book. Then in March 1992, I signed a contract with Addison-Wesley for a work on the fate of the Black Panther Party. I heard that party veteran David Hilliard—once Huey Newton's field marshal—and others, including Bobby Seale, were talking of starting an organization to be called the People's Organized Response (POR), which would "help people at the bottom." For a variety of reasons, not the least of which involved tremendous factionalism between former Black Panthers, POR never got off the ground, but the story I filed about it implied that it would become a reality. The piece referred to the old Black Panther Party in the standard leftist boilerplate and pointed to the federal government's counterintelligence programs as being solely responsible for destroying the party.

Two years later, however, after I began research into the party, something strange began to happen. Despite the leftist credentials I had established, which former Panthers like Landon Williams cited as the reason they talked to me, at least half the people I contacted, including David Hilliard, refused to say anything about the party. Many of the veterans asked me for money as a condition for an interview. Others cited the belief that no one who hadn't been in the party had any business writing about it. In other words, an objective disinterested analysis of the party was out of the question.

Over and over again I was told by veterans that they were writing their own books. After I called to see if she'd agree to an interview, one key female veteran started the process of trying to get a contract to publish her memoirs. Another said she would talk only if I agreed to have my contract rewritten to include her and a black female journalist she had been working with. A close personal friend of Huey's agreed to cooperate when I met with him at the home of Huey's brother Melvin. Melvin Newton himself told me he agreed to meet with me only because I was with Pacific News Service. Huey's close personal friend had been under the impression that I had yet to obtain a book contract. When I traveled to Washington, D.C., to meet with him and informed him that I actually already had the contract in hand, he refused to cooperate.

Despite all of this, key Panthers like Landon Williams did agree to interviews. In addition, my archival research was going quite well at the University of California's Berkeley Bancroft Library, the Library of Congress in Washington, D.C., and the library at the *San Francisco Chronicle*. But still, I felt that something was wrong. I was turning up far too much negative information. As I kept finding things that disproved all the good supposedly done by the party, I looked for something that would restore the organization in my eyes. That something, I decided, was the Black Panther free school in East Oakland, known as the Oakland Community Learning Center. I was convinced that when all was said about the Black Panther fratricide, drug use, infiltration by the government, and so on, the one aspect of the party's operations that could have worked up to this very day as a key element of the "survival program" was the school, although the institution had been closed in 1982 when Huey Newton embezzled money from it and got caught in the act.

I decided I had to tell what the teachers had done and what the young graduates of the school were doing today to leave my readers with the impression that something good was salvageable from the Black Panther legacy. But the leads I was given to anyone who had taught in the school, or administered it, ended up nowhere. Everyone who had had anything to do with the school refused to talk about it, including Erica Huggins, a past principal. In December 1992, I came close to getting someone who had worked there to go into detail about it. But after a deal I was trying to work out with Panther veteran Flores Forbes fell through, this person refused to talk to me.

So with my deadline approaching and my patience with party veterans worn thin, on New Year's Day 1993 I sat down and began to write. Other than eating and sleeping, I didn't do anything but write that manuscript until I was finished. It received good reviews when published and made the front page of the *New York Times Book Review*. This was a good review too, although it reveals something about the hold the mythology of the sixties continues to have on its true believers.

The reviewer selected by the *Times* was Robert Blauner, a professor of sociology at the University of California at Berkeley. He praised my book for going to the heart of the matter about the evil in the Panthers, but he could not keep a hint of outraged romanticism out of his review, particularly when it came to black thuggery. At one point he wrote, "[Pearson] too easily divides black men into solid citizens capable of principled politics and less respectable types who remain criminals even after they achieve revolutionary consciousness. He fails to appreciate how easy it was—for young black men to acquire police records, and how numerous talented blacks find themselves in the criminal subculture."

Here is our problem—and his—in a nutshell. I've been black now for almost thirty-seven years, attended school with other blacks, and know quite a bit about black history. I know for a fact that it is not necessary for blacks to become criminals to prosper. It is precisely Blauner's patronizing romanticism that allowed the Panthers to get away with murder and allows black criminality to flourish today. Although perhaps unconsciously, Blauner expresses perfectly the viewpoint of the fellow-traveling radical of the sixties. Acknowledging that he was part of the "Free Huey" movement after Newton killed police officer John Frey, Blauner says that even though my book shows how several people were murdered by the Panthers while others were sexually abused and beaten within an inch of their lives, he himself does "not regret his involvement" with them—although he now wishes his support had been "more critical." That says it all.

The reviews in the Bay Area were not as good as they were else-where in the country, and I wasn't surprised. While writing in San Francisco I had made plenty of enemies in the media community because I refused to be politically correct. I riled them in particular during the Clarence Thomas/Anita Hill fiasco when in my first column for the *San Francisco Weekly* I simply asked why Hill had continued to work for Thomas if she had been so offended by him; I also encountered antagonism when I accused white feminists as a whole of often engaging in racism. From that point on, I was persona non grata. I predicted to myself that they would be waiting to savage my book if for no better reason than to get me back for past "trans-gressions." My suspicions were confirmed when the *San Francisco Bay Guardian* commissioned Reginald W. Major, a personal friend of many of the Panther veterans criticized in my book, to write a re-view and were further confirmed when the *San Francisco Chronicle Book Review* commissioned the same man to review the book for it too. Major was the only reviewer in the country to savage the book.

It had been a different story a year earlier when Panther veterans Elaine Brown and David Hilliard published their books. *San Francisco Chronicle* book editor Pat Holt had written the front-page re-views of their books herself and didn't say one negative thing about either one of them even though research of her own newspaper's archives would have revealed where many of the lies were, particu-larly in Elaine Brown's memoir. Keeping the faith exacts a stiff price, especially on those who are not quite sure what faith they're keeping.

So now it is August 5, 1995, a little more than a year and a half months since my book came out, and I am answering the taunts of the loud minority of troublemakers here at the Barnes and Noble bookstore in New York City. Most of the audience has enjoyed the reading. But Mr. Ex–Black Panther and a couple of his friends continue to act out, calling me an Uncle Tom, a sellout, and so forth. Officially, they're part of a group that has resurrected the Black Panther newspaper, though its circulation is quite low. According to Mae Jackson, one of my interviewees and a former member of

SNCC, they were sent by Richard "Dhruba" Moore, a Black Panther veteran who went to jail and is now free traveling the nation referring to himself as a former "political prisoner." Moore is one of the veterans I unsuccessfully tried to interview. He's briefly mentioned in my book as a leader of one of the New York City chapters that fell out with Huey, but I say nothing more negative than that. (My focus was not on the East Coast Panthers. If it had been, I would have discussed the connection of "Dhruba" Moore—part of the Eldridge Cleaver faction—with the murder of a Panther named Sam Napier, who was loyal to the Newton faction in the street war between the two Panther branches.) Yet a group Moore is allegedly connected to is passing out leaflets claiming that the FBI hired me to write my book.

Most of the Barnes and Noble audience supports my strong responses to the taunts. At one point I ask, "Who elected the Black Panthers to speak for all of black America?" The hecklers have no answer. After answering the last question and getting a round of applause from most of the audience, I sign about ten copies of my book for those purchasing it. The following day the store manager tells me many more copies were sold to people who just didn't want to buy while the hecklers stood around trying to intimidate them.

In the last sentence of my book I call the Black Panther Party "the quintessential intersection of all the confusion inherent in what it has meant to be African American for the past thirty years." Collectively, we are a confused people—not just African Americans, but the country as a whole. African Americans, I believe, have been left as the most confused of all. Because of our myriad racial strains, we are perhaps the most American of all. Yet we stand on the outside—not only because so many people refuse to see us anywhere else, but also because so many of us refuse to move forward. Too many African Americans are running in place waiting for some external force to provide salvation. Perhaps *The Shadow of the Panther*, which traces the crackup of one of the most grandiose and dangerous of black delusions, sheds some light on how and why we reached such a situation. For our sake, I hope so.

Slipping Through the Crack: Race and the War on Drugs

The five-man crack ring conducted its business with an efficiency an entrepreneur would envy. The group's leader, Christopher Armstrong, would negotiate with customers via a beeper, and after agreeing on an amount and price, he would set up the specifics of the sale. Sometimes he had one of the group's two "runners" deliver the rocks to a prearranged location, but most often the buys took place at the ring's home base, room 203 at La Mirage Motel in Los Angeles, where a cache of .38 caliber and .357 magnum revolvers assured that the transactions would be risk-free.

It was a smooth operation except for one thing. From February to April 1992 informants working on behalf of a joint task force of the Los Angeles police and the federal Bureau of Alcohol, Tobacco, and Firearms made seven visits to room 203 and purchased a total of 124 grams of crack—enough to fuel 1,200 crack pipes. On April 8, members of the task force obtained a warrant and searched the motel room, where they found another 9 grams of crack and a loaded gun. Two of the dealers—Armstrong and runner Aaron

Hampton—were arrested on the spot. The other three members of the gang were apprehended later.

The amount of crack sold and the use of guns made the crimes serious, but in most respects the bust was typical drug business in the Los Angeles ghetto. And when prosecutors in the Central District of California decided to file the case in federal court, they assumed that there would be no problems. But in the years since their arrest, the trial of these alleged dealers—all of whom are black—has become a *cause célèbre* for those who wish to portray the war on drugs as inherently racist due to "disproportionate" sentencing for crack convictions—convictions that are portrayed as unjust and contributing needlessly to the large numbers of black males caught up in the criminal justice system.

These developments began when the Los Angeles County public defender's office accused the federal prosecutors in this case of "selective prosecution"—singling out black defendants for prosecution in federal courts, where crack offenses carry significantly higher sentences, while leaving white users in the state courts to face lesser penalties. As evidence, the county public defender's office pointed out that all twenty-four crack cases handled by the federal court in the Central District in 1991 involved black defendants. The government must show that it did not discriminate against blacks, argued the defense, or the dealers could not be prosecuted. When federal prosecutors balked at being forced to provide information—"discovery," in legal jargon—that would disprove this claim, U.S. District judge Consuelo B. Marshall dismissed the case. Then *United States v. Armstrong* rose to the Supreme Court, and federal policy on crack became a dominant social issue.

The decision facing the Supreme Court in *Armstrong* was limited specifically to the amount of evidence that the defense must provide to require discovery from the government (the court ruled in favor of the government, thereby allowing Armstrong and company to be prosecuted in federal court). Still, the fact that the Supreme Court was asked to make that decision at all signifies how contentious the issue of federal crack sentencing has become. *Armstrong* has already made an impact in the Central District, where more than 130 selective prosecution motions have been filed since Marshall's dismissal of the case.

The argument made by the *Armstrong* defense and other critics—that federal prosecution and sentencing for crack unfairly and unconstitutionally target black defendants—is based on two related, but separate, issues: the disparity in the percentages of black and white defendants prosecuted in federal court and the disparity between the amount of crack and the amount of powder cocaine required to trigger federal mandatory minimum sentences.

The *Armstrong* defense based its claim on the fact that all twenty-four of the federal prosecutions for crack in the Central District of California in 1991 were of black persons. While statistics taken over a longer period of time show that people of other races are also prosecuted under federal crack statutes, a considerable majority of such cases do in fact involve black defendants. For example, from January 1, 1991, through March 31, 1995, 75 percent (109 out of 146) of the defendants prosecuted in federal court for crack in the Central District were black, while during the same period only one white defendant was prosecuted.

Nationally in 1994, the most recent year for which statistics are available, blacks constituted roughly 90 percent of the 3,600 federal crack defendants; whites made up 3.5 percent. According to critics, this "disparate impact" indicates that prosecutors engage in selective prosecution. Furthermore, these critics contend, on average, a defendant convicted in federal court for drug offenses receives a sentence of eighty-six months for trafficking and twenty-two months for possession, compared to thirty-six months and twelve months in the state system. More significantly, say critics of the present system, federal law itself dictates harsher penalties for crack, the form often associated with the black community, than for powder cocaine, the form associated with more affluent white users.

Although the *Armstrong* defense based its claims of selective prosecution solely on the "disparate impact" of federal prosecution, what lies at the heart of the entire debate over federal crack policy is the 100 to 1 ratio mandated by Congress. In practice, the sentences for crack and powder cocaine are somewhat less disparate than the phrase "100 to 1" implies. *The ratio does not refer to the length of sentences but rather to the amount of powder and crack cocaine necessary to trigger the mandatory minimums set down by federal statutes.* The typical sentences for equal amounts of each actually differ at most by a factor of six. For example, a defendant arrested with 50 grams of crack usually receives a sentence of ten years, or about six times the one-and-one-half- to two-year sentence given a defendant caught with 50 grams of powder. For higher amounts, the difference between the penalties diminishes, with upper-level crack defendants receiving a sentence only two times as long as that of powder cocaine dealers.

This equation is a godsend to demagoguery—a shocking statistic that is easily used to convince the uneducated of the authenticity of a weak case. As with the federal prosecution statistics, however, the federal mandate that crack be regarded as more serious than cocaine by a 100 to 1 ratio is actually a reasonable, race-neutral attempt to alleviate the harm done by crack, rather than racism by other means.

When Congress decided on the ratio in 1986, it caused little controversy. Crack was spreading like a cancer in the nation's urban areas. Police departments felt helpless: The drug's low price, quick high, and rapid rate of addiction led to exponential increases in use and trafficking. Drug-related violence skyrocketed everywhere crack gained a foothold, with murder rates increasing as much as 50 percent in some cities.

Manhattan district attorney Robert Morgenthau said that New York City was "drowning" in the drug. Powder cocaine had been a problem, but crack cocaine seemed a different animal. Feeling a sense of urgency, Congress decided to revisit federal anti-drug laws with the idea of giving federal prosecutors additional ammunition against the exploding crack trade. Bob Dole, serving for the first time as Senate majority leader, presented a Reagan Administration plan establishing a powder to crack ratio of 20 to 1 to trigger the mandatory minimum sentences. But as evidence of crack's devastation poured in, legislators decided to get tougher, ratcheting up the penalties for crack to 50 to 1 and then, finally, to the 100 to 1 ratio. In 1988, Congress voted to apply the ratio to possession as well as trafficking cases.

All of the legislation received bipartisan support. Race never became an issue in these deliberations, and many members of the Congressional Black Caucus supported the bills. But times havechanged. Critics of the 100 to 1 ratio now speak in expressly racial terms. Ironically, they consider the ratio discriminatory because crack, according to Berkeley law professor Jerome Skolnick, is "marketed more heavily in minority, especially African-American communities."

This 100 to 1 ratio has caused the brunt of the criticism from academics, politicians, and the popular press. For example, Jesse Jackson has called the statutes "a moral disgrace" that condemn "thousands of young African American and Latino men to languish unjustly in prison." Skolnick described the ratio as "absurd, foolish, and outrageous" and suggested that Congress would be displaying a "racial animus" if it did not amend the law. A *Los Angeles Times* editorial referred to the sentences for crack as "Draconian punishment," and Knoll Lowney, a professor of law at Washington University, wrote that the ratio results in the "overincarceration" of black males and held it responsible for most of the ills of the black community. A Special Report of the U.S. Sentencing Commission released in May 1995 shared these sentiments, recommending that the penalties for crack and powder be made equal.

As these charges attain the status of received truth, their potential implications become clear. At best they suggest that an underlying racism taints the country's war on drugs; at worst they point to a racist government conspiracy of (Johnnie) Cochranesque proportions. But a closer analysis of the prosecution data and of the differences in the impact of crack and powder cocaine suggests that the vast majority of prosecutors, police officers, and legislators base their decisions not on "racial animus" but on the realities of the crack epidemic and those most affected by it.

The critics of the federal policy base their claims solely on the fact that a large majority of federal crack prosecutions—75 percent in the Central District of California and 90 percent nationally—involve black defendants. Because blacks make up such a high percentage of federal crack prosecutions, they argue, federal prosecutors must be taking race into account when they choose whom to try in federal court and whom to leave to the state courts. In other words, at least one of the following must be true: (1) the criteria used to select defendants for federal prosecution must discriminate according to race, or (2) officials must apply guidelines in a racially discriminatory way, having one set of standards for blacks and another for whites.

In fact, the actual guidelines used by the U.S. Attorney's Office in the Central District show that decisions regarding prosecution are neither capricious nor discriminatory. The first guideline concerns the total quantity of crack possessed or distributed by the defendant. The average federal defendant has sold 109 grams of crack, and the overwhelming majority have sold at least 50 grams. Other factors that heavily influence prosecutors' decisions include the defendant's prior felony record and use or possession of a firearm in connection with the crack offense. Membership in a violent street gang or criminal organization, while not sufficient to qualify a defendant for federal prosecution, can also be considered; this factor has particular importance in Los Angeles, where the sale of crack remains in large measure the province of violent gangs. Finally, cases become eligible for federal prosecution in the first place only when federal agencies play a part in the investigation and/or arrest or when state officials bring the case to the U.S. Attorney's attention.

These guidelines hardly form the basis of selective prosecution. (All people, regardless of race, obviously enough, are equally capable of not getting involved with the sale of crack.) In theory, of course, even clearly race-neutral guidelines such as these can be applied in a racially discriminatory manner. But a case-by-case analysis of the federal crack indictments in the Central District between January 1, 1992, and March 31, 1995, suggests that race does not play any role in prosecutorial decisions. Of the 146 defendants charged during this period 94.3 percent either met the quantity requirements, employed firearms, or had prior drug records. All of the cases filed in 1992, 1993, and 1995 qualified for federal prosecution under the quantity guidelines alone. The remaining eight cases involved other aggravating factors such as gang involvement and prior violent felony record.

After looking at these statistics in *United States v. Tyree*, one of the many cases in the wake of *Armstrong* where the defendants filed selective prosecution motions, U.S. District judge Dickran Tevrizian decided that the claims were unfounded: "There is no evidence that the charging decision in any of the cocaine base [i.e., crack] cases . . . was based upon the defendant's race, ethnic origins, or gender, or upon any other impermissible factor."

The same holds true nationwide. Professor John J. DiIulio, of Princeton's Woodrow Wilson School and the Brookings Institute, cites a 1993 study of federal drug sentencing from 1986 to 1990 in concluding that crack cocaine sentencing statutes did not result in racially discriminatory sentences. "The amount of the drug sold," DiIulio wrote, "the offenders' prior criminal records, whether weapons were involved, and other characteristics that federal law and sentencing guidelines established as valid considerations accounted for all the observed variation in sentencing."

If the charges against the U.S. Attorney's Office were true—if "disparate impact" were proof of selective prosecution—one would expect that the state courts would be full of white crack offenders who were passed over for federal prosecution by racially biased prosecutors. The facts do not bear this out. A study of federal and state crack defendants between January 1, 1990, and August 11, 1992, shows no evidence that prosecutors allowed whites eligible for federal prosecution to remain in the state courts.

That the high number of black federal crack defendants is not the result of discrimination may seem surprising only to the Jesse Jacksons of this world. Statistics concerning prosecution for drugs other than crack compiled by the Central District Pretrial Services Office over the past three years indicate that out of the total number of federal drug defendants, 50 percent were Hispanic, 25 percent were black, 17 percent were white, and 7.5 percent were Asian.

Viewed separately, each particular drug has its own "disparate impact." Almost 63 percent of powder cocaine defendants were Hispanic, a percentage that would increase dramatically if fugitives who fled the country before being interviewed by Pretrial Services were included. The feds prosecuted more Asians than blacks for heroin, and seven times as many whites as blacks for methamphetamines ("crank"). Whites represented over 64 percent of marijuana defendants, and over 85 percent of LSD defendants, drugs for which no blacks were indicted over the three-year period.

If selective prosecution were inferred from these figures, one would have to conclude that whites are victimized in LSD cases, Hispanics in powder cocaine cases, and so on. One would have to go further and say that whites are victims of racially motivated prosecutions in child pornography, antitrust, securities fraud, insider trading, and defense-contractor fraud cases.

As Princeton politics professor Robert George points out, the notion that statistical disparity on its face indicates selective prosecution would justify cries of discrimination in literally any legal circumstance. A former member of the Civil Rights Commission, George notes ironically that even though surveys indicate that evangelical Christians represent 36 percent of the American population, he does not know of any in the fifty-member department of politics where he works: "I would be very happy, if we are going to decide that disparate impact is evidence of discrimination, to make the argument that my department, Ivy League universities, and the prestige universities in general are discriminating against evangelicals."

Despite the elaborate conspiracy theories held by critics of national drug policy, statistical and anecdotal evidence suggest that federal crack prosecution figures result from the real-world demographics of crack rather than from racial discrimination. Few people would dispute the idea that blacks make up a large percentage of crack abusers. Even fewer would disagree that crack has wreaked its worst havoc in the black community. As the *Los Angeles Times* reported in a 1994 series on the crack epidemic, "for a variety of social reasons, the drug has burned its greatest swath through low-income, mostly minority neighborhoods, where for only $5 or $10 it offers in concentrated form a high [otherwise] available only to those who could afford costly powder cocaine."

Furthermore, the dealers who sell crack within the black community are overwhelmingly black as well. In a sworn declaration submitted to the 9th Circuit Court of Appeals in *Armstrong*, Special Agent Ralph Lochridge of the U.S. Drug Enforcement Administration testified that certain ethnic groups tend to be involved with certain types of illegal drugs. "With respect to cocaine base [crack]," Lochridge testified, "virtually all major crack traffickers uncovered in the Los Angeles area have been black and operate primarily in black neighborhoods."

And there is no doubt whatsoever that the presence of crack in the black community has been catastrophic. Retired Circuit Court judge Edward Rogers, who thirty years ago became one of the first black judges in the state of Florida and later established the first drug courts in Palm Beach County, says that crack "weaves its way throughout all of the ills that are suffered in the black community." He adds, "I think that if you look into child abuse or spousal abuse or crimes of violence or crimes of larceny or almost 90 percent of any kind of crime you would find drug abuse and crack cocaine in particular at the bottom of it."

No one accuses crack of being an equal-opportunity destroyer. Like the street gangs that make their living selling it, crack has worked its way into—and does most of its damage in—low-income urban black communities, where its influence is abetted by other social pathologies. Given this situation, says Professor Bryan A. Liang of Pepperdine Law School, it makes sense that prosecutors and law enforcement officials should focus their attention in dealing with crack in at-risk communities. Liang characterizes the decision as an economic rather than a racial one: "In a world like ours in which you have limited resources, you have to go into the communities which are most affected by the criminal activity. For crack that would be the urban communities. . . . So you have to go there. You have to go where the crime is. You can't pick and choose on the basis of race where to prosecute in order to be 'fair.' You have to use your resources to get rid of the most crime possible."

U.S. Attorney Nora Manella calls this kind of resource allocation "both rational and constitutional" and compares it to other decisions law enforcement makes. "Just as law enforcement concentrates white collar fraud resources in the business community," she explains, "it concentrates resources devoted to curbing the manufacture and wholesale trafficking of crack and its attendant violence in those areas whose citizens are most at risk from that criminal activity."

There was a time, remembers UCLA professor James Q. Wilson, when Jesse Jackson and the civil rights establishment wanted police officers to pay more attention to the crack trade in black neighborhoods. "If the police walked by a crack dealer standing on a black neighborhood street corner, the police would be criticized by residents, law professors, and others for ignoring visible drug dealing," he says. "Now they are cracking down . . . and they are being accused of 'overincarcerating' blacks. The people who make these accusations have to answer the following question: What is the 'right' level of prosecution for crack cocaine?"

Legal scholar Henry Mark Holzer, recently retired from his professorship at Brooklyn Law School, would ask a slightly different question. "Do these critics want the blacks who sell crack to go free, or do they want to force whites to sell crack so that they can go to jail in equal numbers? It's ridiculous! Who can take this seriously?"

Jesse Jackson and his allies in the onslaught on U.S. drug policy may waver in their desire to see crack dealers prosecuted, but the people who actually live in the areas most affected by the drug do not share their ambivalence. In fact, according to Los Angeles County Sheriff Sherman Block, who has been a law enforcement officer all his working life, police usually direct their efforts in response to citizens' requests. "Usually it is complaints from the residents of the area," he explains. "There is a crack house there, and because of the people who frequent it, they are afraid to let their children out."

The residents—particularly the children—have suffered the most. While the civil rights establishment has rallied on behalf of drug pushers in the cynical effort to prove America a racist society, crack has taken their neighborhoods away from them.

Bryan Liang, who prior to becoming a law professor saw the effects of crack up close as an emergency room physician in the Washington Heights area of New York City, has little patience for those who seem to think that crack prosecution should be conducted according to affirmative action quotas. "People in these communities are being ravaged by this drug," he says. "There is this idea that it is 'unfair' to prosecute these black dealers. Well it is unfair that these black dealers are preying upon blacks in those communities. We should be thinking about the victims."

It is obvious that crack does the most damage in communities where the dealers, addicts, and innocent bystanders happen to be black. U.S. Attorney Nora Manella calls the focus on these areas "the functional equivalent of putting traffic cops at the busiest intersections, because that is where the greatest risk of the greatest harm to the greatest number of people lies."

What about the sentences in these cases? Are they unfair? The average federal crack defendant has been arrested with 109 grams of crack, which can translate into as many as 1,090 individual doses and as much as $12,500. And contrary to the claim that the sentences punish addicts, and not dealers, the overwhelming majority of federal defendants have been arrested for trafficking as opposed to simple possession. According to the U.S. Bureau of Justice statistics, for example, in 1994 dealers accounted for 98.2 percent of federal crack convictions.

Those who defend the 100 to 1 ratio for triggering minimum sentences argue that the comparison between crack and cocaine is chemically as well as legally justified. Because of crack's high concentration and the fact that it is smoked rather than snorted, it tends to be much more addictive than powder. Crack reaches the brain sixteen times faster than powder—in about nineteen seconds—and the drug takes its effect in one-twentieth the time. The resulting high is both more intense and shorter-lasting than that of a powder—a high that translates into more frequent bingeing, and a quicker psychological addiction.

Retired Circuit Court judge Edward Rogers says this feature makes crack particularly dangerous.

"I know a lot of people who did powder cocaine socially at parties, or once a month, or once every three months, or every now and then, and they could take it or leave it," he says. "I don't know many people who have experimented like that with crack. The crack dealers will give you stuff [for free] to get you hooked. It is just so addictive."

People who work with those in the throes of crack addiction say the same thing. Marva Mitchem is the executive director at Restore, a center providing housing and treatment for women in South Central Los Angeles. When asked what crack dependency is like, the diminutive black woman leans forward in her chair and looks right into her listener's eyes so that there will be no misunderstanding. "They say you have no sense of self," she explains. "You would sell your soul, sell your own mother for one hit of crack. It has that much power over you."

Crack's increasingly close association with violence also seems to set it apart from traditional cocaine. As mentioned earlier, drug-related violent crime increased all over the country when crack hit the scene, with murder rates going up in some cities by 50 percent. The U.S. Sentencing Commission made note of this unique aspect of the crack epidemic in the report it delivered to Congress in 1995 when it said that "crack dealers generally tend to have a stronger association with systemic violence [violence associated with the marketing of a drug] and are more likely to possess weapons than [are] powder cocaine dealers."

In addition to increasing the level of violence in the community, says Sheriff Sherman Block, "we saw a whole new kind of violence. Not only did the incidence of violence go up, the nature of the violence changed in that we were witnessing more random violence, violence seemingly for the sake of violence."

The close relationship between crack and violent crime exacts other social costs as well. The health care costs associated with crack use astound. The number of cocaine-related medical emergencies in the United States has increased 500 percent since 1983, with crack largely responsible for the rise. The high potency of the drug causes some users to suffer severe internal organ damage. Treatment for drug-exposed infants, the vast majority of whom had been exposed to crack, cost Los Angeles County public hospitals approximately $22 million in 1991 alone. An individual case of crack exposure—there are over 2,000 in the county each year—can cost anywhere from $8,000 to over $200,000 per child.

The desperate addiction associated with the drug has made "strawberries"—prostitutes who work for crack—fixtures of the crack culture. According to one estimate the AIDS rate in crack-infested areas can reach as high as one in five residents. Crack has also made a major contribution to homelessness in the nation's cities. In some locations estimates indicate that as much as 80 percent of the local homeless population uses crack.

Low prices help fuel the boom and make crack's intense high—and quick addiction—available to just about anyone. Sold in doses as small as one-tenth of a gram, crack can be had for as little as two dollars. Michael Reed, a drug abuse counselor at Southern

California Alcohol and Drug Programs, Inc., says that the drug's low cost explains its high concentration in low-income neighborhoods. "It's an addict's dream and a society's nightmare," he says, "a cheap high. It's extremely addictive and extremely inexpensive, which takes it right into poor areas and keeps it there."

Even the youngest members of those communities can afford a rock that costs less than a McDonald's Happy Meal. Reed goes so far as to say that "crack was designed for a school-aged child. A child can save his lunch money and by Friday have enough money to get loaded all weekend."

Powder cocaine, to be sure, takes a heavy toll on its users, but it does not seem to have the devastating, community-wide impact that crack does. George Mason University economics chairman Walter Williams, who is black, remarks that "people out in the suburbs using powder cocaine don't see the kind of stuff going on that you see in the inner cities with the use of crack."

Powder cocaine's higher price, lower potency, and lower addictive qualities may explain this. In addition, suggests Professor Liang, the demographics of those who use the two drugs magnify the differences between crack and cocaine.

A drug of the middle and upper classes, "powder cocaine definitely has an effect on those individuals, but they have social structures that they can fall back upon. They have more stable family lives, they aren't as desperate. . . . The people who use crack are so close to the edge [in economic and social terms] that crack just pushes them over."

In the words of Sister Alice Callaghan, director of the Las Familias del Pueblo family service agency in Los Angeles, "When you are disadvantaged and you throw crack into that, you absolutely can't make it. . . . Crack just crumbles you. It pins you to the ground."

Given crack's effects on both the user and the surrounding community and the fact that it is pandemic in the black ghetto, it would actually seem to be racist *not* to punish its sale more severely than we punish the sale of other drugs.

AFRO-FASCISM

AFRO-FASCISM

Afro-Fascism on the Rise

When Michael Hethmon, a resident of Prince Georges County, Maryland, read in a local paper that an "Afrocentric Exposition" was going to be held at his local Largo High School, his curiosity was piqued. He knew that multicultural education was much in vogue in the state and that Afrocentrism in particular was being vigorously championed in the Prince Georges County public school system, where a majority of the students are black. Hethmon had long been interested in the study of African civilization. And since he was the father of a baby girl who would be entering the local school system in a few years, he wanted to know more about the reforms that were transforming local elementary and secondary education. He decided to go to the exposition.

Arriving at Largo High School on the morning of December 1, 1990, Hethmon found that the workshops had just ended. About thirty people were still milling around in the lobby, evidently following up on discussions initiated in the workshop sessions. Asking about the exposition display, Hethmon was directed toward a pair of tables, one covered with badges, kente cloth, and other assorted items currently in fashion among enthusiasts of African culture, and the other with books and pamphlets.

Unable to find the books intended for classroom use, Hethmon began to browse through some of the designated "adult" texts, which evidently had been written primarily for an audience of teachers and other pedagogues in Afrocentric programs. What he read jolted him. Official promotional literature on the Maryland state multicultural program had consistently stressed "inclusiveness" and "respect for a diversity of cultural heritages," but the books that Hethmon found didn't reflect these aims. He encountered what he would later describe as "some of the most bigoted, twisted, hateful material I have seen in years." Slurs against Jews and Americans of European, Asian, and mixed-race ancestry; assertions of the genetic, cultural, and moral superiority of "Afrikans"; and exhortations to fight against integration and racial intermarriage were combined with extremely dubious historical and religious doctrines in a "conspiracy theory" format eerily similar to that used by racist and fascist organizations such as the Ku Klux Klan and American Nazi Party.

One book in the display especially dismayed Hethmon and remained with him as a symbol of Afrocentric hate literature; in the months ahead, as he waged a lonely struggle against the Maryland educational bureaucracy to purge the curriculum of bigotry, he would show it to those who claimed that critics of radical Afrocentrism were exaggerating the problem or themselves being racist. The book was titled *The Black Student's Guide to Positive Education* and was written by Baba Zak Kondo, who is identified as director of the International Studies Program and a teacher of history at Bowie State University in Maryland. The book comes with the usual catalogue of enthusiastic endorsements, chief among them a back-cover blurb from the director of the University of Virginia's African American Cultural Center that characterizes Kondo's work as "a detailed and philosophical approach, rooted in African American Culture, to effective leadership styles for Black Administrators and student leaders."

Yet Hethmon did not have to read far to discover that something more than simple leadership training was on the author's mind. "This essay is designed to combat the miseducation of Black students," Kondo states in the preface. "Most whites and their satellites—Negroes—will find this essay unnecessary at best, anti-white at worst. Neither finding will be accurate." Then he launches into a diatribe against the hypothetical black man who accepts the values of "white Amerika" and succeeds in mainstream society. "Tom," Kondo's hypothetical villain in the book's opening chapter, recites the Pledge of Allegiance in school every morning, volunteers for the military out of a misguided patriotic zeal, wins admission into Johns Hopkins Medical School, does his residency at a "lily-white hospital in suburban Maryland," marries a white woman, moves into a white neighborhood, and joins a white club.

"By Amerikan standards, Tom is a success," Kondo summarizes; but by "Black standards, Tom is a disgrace. A misfit. A sickening soul. An 'Oreo.' A mental time bomb waiting to explode." He is an "ogre that Amerikan education clones *en masse*. This creature must be mentally aborted if young Blacks in this country are to free their minds from mental slavery."

This preoccupation with blacks who break rank and deny the summons to racial solidarity is at the core of *The Black Student's Guide*. Returning again to the problem of the "Negroes" who study the Founding Fathers ("some of the most racist, inhumane, immoral men ever to live") and who are thereby suckered into accepting the American political and economic system, Kondo castigates college-educated blacks who "sell out the Afrikan masses for money, material gain, or position." "In a very real sense," he says, "these individuals are *traitors*. As a race, we can no longer tolerate traitors in our community."

Hethmon was dismayed by the rant in the book but even more disturbed by the fantasy about "Afrikan" history. Kondo holds that Afrikans (and the term always refers to black Africans, not to Arabs or other inhabitants of the African continent) were the first humans, the first Europeans, the inhabitants of Sumer, the original Egyptians, the original Jews, the original Greeks, and the original Italians. Moreover, Beethoven was Afrikan, along with Alexander Hamilton (his

status as a Founding Father notwithstanding), Pushkin, Robert
Browning, Saint Jerome, and the prophet Mohammed's maternal
grandmother. Afrikans discovered farming, invented literacy, and created at Luxor the world's first university; and Ghana, Mali, and Song-
hay created the "first modern nations on this planet." Indeed Africa
was the "epitome of civilizations" in times when "western Europe
lived in a state of savagery and barbarity" featuring "filth, sexual disease, incest, homosexuality, bestiality, and anarchy." The nemesis of
black people is and always has been the white man, who "continues
to exploit, degrade, and oppress Afrikans (and other non-whites) at
every corner of the globe. To recognize this fact does not make you
anti-white or racist. It merely means that you have enough intelligence to know your *enemy.* . . . The white man is our enemy. As a result, his interests and our interests can never be the same just as the
interest of the master and the slave can never be the same." Kondo
stresses the need to recognize that, at a certain point, "you must resort
to violence to protect and defend yourself and your people. If and
when this becomes necessary, do not compromise on this challenge."

Poring over page after page of this material, Hethmon was
appalled. It was shocking enough that someone would write material
of this kind and that someone else would publish it. But what could
possibly be the justification, he wondered, for imposing such bigotry
on impressionable elementary and high school students? On what
basis could young black students, learning about their worlds for the
first time, critically evaluate a version of history and race relations
that would pit them in a lifelong struggle against the white race? And
how would white students feel in a school system where they were
depicted as enemies against whom violence might be needed?

What made the official endorsement of such racist antiwhite
tracts in the school system particularly gratuitous was the fact that
Prince Georges County, unlike the neighboring District of Columbia, has not been weighed down by an urban underclass that might
be assumed to be too unsophisticated to evaluate material such as

that presented by Kondo. Located along the northeast corner of the Beltway in the Washington metropolitan area, the county has an unusually high concentration of educated and comparatively prosperous black professionals, many of whom commute to work in the nation's capital. Boasting mean and median annual household incomes of $43,127 and $48,606 respectively, Prince Georges is, in fact, among the wealthiest counties in Maryland. Blacks constitute 50.7 percent of the overall county population (whites constitute 43.1 percent), but in the public school system there is a 67 percent to 23 percent black-white ratio. In 1993 the county school system was the fifteenth largest in the nation.

As Michael Hethmon began to research the issue, he learned that multicultural education in Maryland first gained momentum in the late 1960s, with a 1969 Maryland State Department of Education bylaw establishing the first multicultural guidelines. Nothing more was done for the next twenty years; but then, in 1987, with multiculturalism transformed into a militant movement and on the rise nationally, the Prince Georges County Board of Education established a task force on multicultural education. In its report, submitted and accepted in the following year, the task force urged a modification of existing curricula so as to promote greater awareness of the history and cultural contributions of the diverse groups that make up the American population at large. The language of the multicultural initiative stressed such virtues as tolerance and inclusiveness. Indeed, they were required by the 1969 statewide multicultural guidelines, which had expressly called for a curriculum encouraging respect for cultural diversity and "eliminating stereotypes related to racial, ethnic, and cultural groups." Promotional literature on Prince Georges County multicultural education featured themes such as "successful learning for all students," "quality and equity," and respect for "ethnic heritage."

Plainly these benign characterizations of Prince Georges County multicultural education did not jibe with the reality, if the books and pamphlets on the exposition display table were any indicator of what county educators had in mind. Hethmon himself was well disposed toward a genuine multiculturalism, having majored in Near Eastern Studies at UCLA in the early 1980s and having cultivated fluency in Arabic during two years' study at the Institute Bourguiba in Tunisia and American University in Cairo. From the perspective of one with some real interest in and acquaintance with world cultural history, the Prince Georges County version of "multiculturalism" seemed nothing short of a fraud.

Determined not to let this program pass without public scrutiny, Hethmon returned home from the exhibition and wrote a formal letter of complaint to the office of the superintendent of schools. In it he pointed out that since the Afrocentric Exposition had been held on public school property, advertised through the Office of Public Affairs and Communications, and sponsored by the two members of the county education board, in effect the board was condoning it: "The logical lack of formal sanction for the promotion of bigotry, hate, and violence in no way absolves the Board of Education of the responsibility for this incident. . . . To fail to condemn hate doctrines or their promotion, particularly in a public institution, is morally, politically and legally equivalent to tolerating them." In response, Warren Simmons, a special assistant to the superintendent, acknowledged that the Kondo book did indeed seem to foster bigotry, and he invited Hethmon to serve on the Multicultural Education Materials Evaluation Committee, comprising eight school district employees and three community representatives. The committee was charged with ensuring that the proposed classroom instructional materials complied with state guidelines, and with recommending material to the Board of Education.

Relieved that the system seemed to be rational and responsive after all, Hethmon accepted the invitation and attended the first meeting of the committee on January 26, 1991. To his dismay he found that the committee had been largely packed with militant black activists and that the Kondo book, far from representing an aberration, was one in a list of books under consideration for inclusion in the "must have" list for school libraries. When Hethmon spoke out in protest, a decision about the matter was deferred until the next meeting. On January 31, the superintendent's office informed members of the committee that $500,000 had been allocated for immediate expenditure on these multicultural materials and that the committee should be prepared to submit its recommendations within two weeks—or a month at the outside. When Hethmon protested that such deadlines would leave him with little time to procure and read copies of the books in question, he was told that he ought to realize that "white people were now a minority in the world," that "the future belongs to people of color," and that, in insisting on his right to review the books, he was trying to "censor the thoughts and control the minds" of young blacks. When Hethmon pointed out that many persons in the community would be alienated by materials of this kind, another committee member said, "We don't know who these people are, and we don't even consider them because they don't matter."

Despite the sharp edge of this encounter, Hethmon embarked on a crash course on Afrocentric literature during the spring of 1991. Because the debate over political correctness was erupting in the national media at this time, the Afrocentric movement and its intellectual paraphernalia were receiving considerable attention. This was partly in consequence of the first draft of the so-called Sobol Report (ultimately published as *One Nation, Many Peoples* by the New York State Department of Education later in the year), which held that the traditional social sciences were "racist," and partly as a result of the antics of Leonard Jeffries, former chairman of the African American Studies program at the City University of New York and an exponent of the "melanin" theory of white genetic inferiority.

Yet despite the adverse publicity and the farcical nature of many of its claims, the Afrocentrism movement continued to spread, and Afrocentric curricula were in place or under consideration in many major cities and school districts throughout the country. An important source text for these initiatives, Hethmon discovered, was a collection inspired and edited by Asa Hilliard, the African American Baseline Essays. This collection, a source for writers like Kondo, holds that most of the significant accomplishments of early humans originated in black Africa. Black Africans in ancient times pioneered the science of electrical engineering, developed gliders or "sailplanes," and contributed to the cultural milieu that produced the first steam engine in the second century B.C. A major center of such cultural and scientific advances was Egypt, which the Baseline Essays flatly characterize as a black civilization, as though this were a fact established beyond dispute. Indeed, Egypt is said to have been the source of the discoveries and insights that have hitherto been attributed to Plato, Aristotle, and other Greek philosophers, which leads inescapably to the conclusion that the intellectual and philosophical foundations of Western civilization were borrowed or plundered from the black Africans.

Hethmon could see that the assumptions of this revisionist view of ancient history—present not only in the Baseline Essays but also in more "scholarly" texts such as G. M. James's *Stolen Legacy* and Cheik Anta Diop's *Nations nègres et culture*, which were published three or four decades ago and have now acquired something of the status of cult classics—was spreading outward into the "mainstream."

As Hethmon followed through the line of footnotes, many of which kept referring in circular fashion back and forth until what had originated as unsupported assertions had acquired the aura of legitimacy, he became aware that the "scholarly" and more "popular" forms of Afrocentrism were virtually identical. One influential collection of essays, *Infusion of African and African American Content in the School Curriculum*, opens with an essay by Ivan van Sertima, founding editor of *The Journal of African Civilization*, which holds that "Africans" were among the original inhabitants of pre-Roman Britain, among the Vikings who discovered the New World, among the ancient Chinese ("the first emperor of China was a black man"), and even among the Japanese samurai. White Europeans came into being when the black

Africans who first explored the region were caught in the ice during the Ice Age and lost the melanin in their skin pigment due to the blockage of the sun. This explanation jibes nicely with Leonard Jeffries' more vulgarly expressed melanin theory, according to which the differences between blacks, who as "sun people" are warm, empathetic, and community-minded, and whites, who as "ice people" are analytic, individualistic, and violent, can be related to the presence or absence of melanin in the skin. Indeed, van Sertima cites Jeffries with approval.

As he read further, Hethmon discovered that pseudobiological and evolutionary arguments of this type seem to be enjoying growing currency in Afrocentric circles. According to black psychiatrist Frances Cress Welsing, for example, white racism is psychogenetic in origin, since white people, when they intermarry with other races, produce colored offspring. Terrorized by the prospect of "genetic annihilation" (a sad fate that is represented, evidently, in the failure to produce a child of one's own color), white people feel obligated to adopt a militant posture vis-à-vis the nonwhite races of the world. Even Adolf Hitler's anti-Semitism was, according to Welsing, at root a variant of the same antiblack prejudice. Jews are actually mulattos, dark-skinned, kinky-haired; in trying to exterminate them, Hitler was merely conducting another battle in the age-old white campaign for genetic survival in a world dominated by people of color.

This preoccupation with racial and genetic purity, a preoccupation that Welsing attributes to white people, appears in another form in Chancellor Williams's *The Destruction of Black Civilization*, one of the most frequently cited and highly praised of the recent Afrocentric texts. According to Williams, black civilization in central Africa and Egypt was subverted by guileful whites who intermarried and produced "bastard offspring," who then turned against black people as an expression of their own self-hatred. "Asians," to Williams, are a mixed breed who ally themselves with whites in an ongoing conspiracy to destroy black civilization and all record of its achievements. This conspiratorial theme is a constant in Williams's history, which begins in ancient Egypt ("Ethiopia's oldest daughter"), continues with an account of central African civilizations after the "scattering of the people," chronicles the arrival of European colonialists (or "white devils from the West"), and concludes with exhortations toward modern-day black unity. Williams writes, "The necessary re-education of Blacks and a possible solution of the racial crisis can begin . . . only when Blacks fully realize this central fact in their lives: the white man is their *Bitter Enemy*. For this is not the ranting of wild-eyed militancy, but the calm and unmistakable verdict of several thousand years of documented history."

By the time he had read through these materials, Michael Hethmon was convinced that the racism that had so dismayed him at the exposition was not confined to a few texts like Kondo's that could be eliminated from the list of classroom instructional materials but was at the very heart of contemporary Afrocentric thought. He believed that the Prince Georges County proponents of multicultural education could not fail to know this. Yet they had shown themselves determined nonetheless to proceed with an infusion of Afrocentrism into the curriculum, suggesting that they themselves were sympathetic to the racial separatist and black supremacist Afrocentric agenda.

Because of the apparently monolithic opposition he faced, Hethmon realized that he could not respond globally to the genesis and dissemination of Afrocentrist mythology. If he did that, he reasoned, he would be seen as putting forth a view that could be dismissed as the mirror image of the Afrocentrists' twisted facts and paranoid reasoning. So he decided to concentrate on a clinical evaluation of two books, Diop's *The Origin of Black Civilization* and Williams's *The Destruction of Black Civilization*, and over the next two years he filed a series of complaints with county and state agencies, citing numerous passages in these books that denigrated and stereotyped whites, Jews, and Asians.

In March 1991, Hethmon submitted a discrimination complaint under Title VI of the Civil Rights Act. A month later he filed a "request for reconsideration of library or classroom instructional materials." A hearing was scheduled for late May; Hethmon was given fifteen minutes at the hearing to set forth his arguments against the inclusion of the Diop and Williams books on the "must have" lists for school libraries. Since the county multicultural program uses no formal textbooks, these lists of approved instructional materials are particularly crucial, because they establish the resource bank on which teachers draw in presenting the subject matter to their students.

The evaluation committee's subsequent decision and report was a preview of the obfuscation and evasiveness that Hethmon was to encounter, time and again, in his dealings with the county educational establishment over the ensuing months and years. Hethmon's complaints were without merit, the committee determined, partly because the Diop and Williams books had been favorably reviewed in several publications, but more fundamentally because, as books approved for library use and not for the classroom per se, "they do not necessarily reflect the multicultural definition and perspective of the Prince Georges County Public Schools." According to the committee, the fact that the school libraries contain copies of *Mein Kampf*, the Bible, and the Koran "does not imply the adoption of Nazism, Christianity, or Islam as part of the curriculum." Further, students ought not to be kept in ignorance of the existence of Afrocentric theory and the Afrocentric movement but should, on the contrary, be given access to and encouraged to explore "multiple points of view."

Hethmon's response was that he would never have protested Kondo's *Guide* if it had been intended for use alongside *Mein Kampf* as an example of the hate literature that students should learn to recognize and deplore. And unlike the Koran, for example, Afrocentrism as expressed in texts like Kondo's was part of the multicultural mandate. He pointed out the problem as he saw it: The Afrocentric hatred of and paranoia about white people is very much a contemporary reality among those segments of the population that are attracted to this literature, and in validating these works the school system had given no indication that it repudiated this particular form of racism.

In arguing his case, Hethmon pointed out that the distinction between studying a racist screed as a significant (if benighted) social phenomenon, on the one hand, and teaching it as "truth" on the other hand, is an obvious one that the committee members surely must grasp. If the prohibition against racial denigration and stereotyping that had been mandated in the multicultural guidelines did not apply to such material, what force did these guidelines have? These guidelines were very much in force—and rightly so—where white supremacist literature was concerned, none of which had been in evidence in the curriculum for decades. In short, he concluded, the committee seemed to be endorsing a racial double standard and concealing this double standard by its recourse to the language of "access" and diversity of viewpoint.

When his arguments were rejected, Hethmon wrote a letter of protest at the beginning of June to Associate Superintendent Louise Waynant, who replied that he would be given an opportunity to present a formal appeal. But in September, after a series of delays, Waynant wrote again to explain that there would be no formal review of the objectionable materials after all, but only a formal vote on their adoption. Meanwhile, the list of "must have" books and materials that the committee had earlier approved had, without Hethmon's knowledge, been altered to include new Afrocentric tracts favored by another militant evaluation committee member. This revised (and further racialized) list was approved in a final evaluation committee meeting of October 24, after which the committee was effectively disbanded. This allowed for the transfer of its functions to venues within the Office of Equity Assurance that could proceed without the inconvenience of Hethmon's dissent.

In that final meeting, nonetheless, Hethmon filed nine pages of detailed review and citation from the Williams and Diop books. More than two months later, Waynant notified him that despite his objections, she had approved the committee's recommendations. Hethmon appealed again, this time to Superintendent Edward Felegy, who rejected his appeal eight months later, on August 19,

1992, and upheld the recommendation of the advisory committee, although he did so without holding the public hearing required by the public school laws of Maryland.

Hethmon then put the matter before Suzanne Plogman, chair of the Prince Georges County Board of Education, who again rejected his complaint without responding to Hethmon's substantive objection—that the objectionable material was "racist pornography" whose "primary purpose is to incite and encourage racist and anti-Semitic stereotypes and emotions."

Undaunted, Hethmon wrote a twenty-three-page letter of appeal to Nancy Grasmick, the state superintendent of education. In response, the Prince Georges County Board of Education applied for a summary affirmation that would dismiss the appeal without the necessity of a public hearing. The board's statement and an accompanying affidavit by Associate Superintendent Waynant followed the precedent of previous county responses in their refusal to deal with the fundamental problems that Hethmon had been pointing to. Indeed, virtually none of the county representatives had at any point acknowledged that Williams, Diop, Kondo, or other Afrocentric writers might conceivably be racist or that whites in their school district might object to being characterized—purely on the basis of their skin color—as oppressors, bigots, and enemies of the black race.

While this legalistic maneuvering was still in progress, the Prince Georges County Alliance of Black Educators, as if to register disdain for this lonely critic of the Afrocentric movement, sponsored another conference, this time on "saving the African American child through educational and cultural excellence." Held at Central High School in Capitol Heights on May 30, 1992, the conference was attended by some three hundred educators, including such notables as Prince Georges County schools superintendent Edward Felegy and a Democratic candidate for Congress.

For Michael Hethmon, the highlight of the conference was the final workshop, "Rites of Passage," which used as its primary source material an article by one of the workshop facilitators, Nsenda

Warfield-Coppock. This article designated as its three objectives to increase knowledge of (1) "the role of the brain in cultural memory," (2) "the uniqueness of African people based on melanin," and (3) "the role of the pineal gland in access to cultural memory."

According to Warfield-Coppock, melanin "balances or keeps the central nervous system functioning at an optimal level." For this reason, African American infants, who are blessed with more melanin than whites, "are more advanced in intelligence and motor skills than are children of lighter-skinned races or ethnic groups." Melanin helps black athletes "glide through the air like Magic Johnson or Michael Jordan, or hit top speeds like Florence Griffith-Joyner and Carl Lewis." Because of their high melanin levels people of darker skin are better able to access the "cultural memory banks" and get in touch with spiritual "energy and vibrations from the environment." Warfield-Coppock concluded that access to this new scientific information, long suppressed by European scholars, would help black youths develop a sense of self and recover an awareness of their native talents. Even more crucial than melanin as a cause of black superiority, however, is the pineal gland, which "appears to be highly active in people of color." The pineal gland enables one to sense "etheric vibrations" and to "see and feel what is not visible or concrete." Among white people, unfortunately, the pineal gland calcifies between 30 and 60 percent of the time, which makes whites not only less perceptive but also more disposed toward sexual perversion and sexual violence. ("The prison population of gruesome sexual crime is approximately 97 percent white, with sometimes as many as a third of incarcerated white American men in any given prison being there for sexual offenses.")

By contrast, black people whose pineal glands are functioning well are particularly sensitive to "feelings or perceptions of discrimination, feelings of prejudice." This is why "young African American children may have difficulty in a school setting." Even those (presumably white) teachers who "espouse objectivity toward children of color cannot hide their feelings," feelings which those hypersensitive pineal-enriched children can intuit without being told. Since the causes of white insensitivity are seen as biological, one is led to infer that racial integration has no future in the world of Afrocentric education.

Hethmon came away from this new chapter in Afrocentrism feeling that he had just been released after spending some time in a spaceship. It increased his desire to do something and also his fear that this development had now achieved critical mass in his community. With the county and state educational bureaucracies both unresponsive and intimidated, he sought legal help from the Washington-based Center for Individual Rights, which has over the past few years given support to many others struggling against the tyranny of the academic and intellectual Left.

In August 1993, a Center for Individual Rights attorney appeared on Hethmon's behalf before the state Board of Education. The board was not pleased at the prospect of validating an Afrocentric coup, but even more wary of becoming embroiled in a local educational issue. After deliberations, its members decided not to order changes in Prince Georges County's curriculum.

For some, this decision indicated that the determined twenty-year effort on the part of the state of Maryland to achieve racial balance and equity in the state's public schools was over. Critics of the Board of Education's decision believed that its stand would cause white flight out of the Prince Georges schools and set the state back to the era before *Brown v. Board of Education*. They suspect, moreover, that this is exactly the outcome that proponents of Afrocentrism hope for.

The crusade has not made Michael Hethmon feel noble or righteous. Coming to an ambiguous end, it has been a lonely and painful trek with little support from other parents and much antagonism from the educational bureaucracy. Every time Hethmon looks at his daughter, who will start school soon, he thinks about melanin and pineal glands and ancient black aviators in Stone Age gliders and knows that he is caught in a surrealistic dream that will end only when everyone else wakes up.

Making Black Supremacist NOIse

In the summer of 1930, an itinerant peddler arrived in Detroit's black ghetto, selling silk fabrics and mystical theories of black supremacy from door to door. Calling himself Wali Fard Muhammad, this proponent of racial Armageddon claimed to be a prince of Mecca, the original Afro-Asiatic black man of the tribe of Shabazz, first humans and creators of civilization. He had come to release his people from bondage in the wilderness of the white man's America, for he actually was, as he later told confidants, Allah, God Himself, in human form. Light-skinned, Caucasian in features, and with eyes described as "maroon," Fard Muhammad's eerie appearance led some to say he was an Arab or Hispanic, passing himself off as a mulatto. He claimed this appearance was necessary to be able to travel unhindered in racist America. He gathered enough believers that he was soon able to found a militantly racist pseudoreligion, the Nation of Islam (NOI).

Whatever else he was or wasn't, Wali Fard Muhammad was no musician. Yet his teachings would become, more than sixty years later, the single most important nonmusical influence on contemporary rappers, inspiring many of them to become little more than propagandists for the cult he founded—while enriching themselves in the process. Public Enemy, Poor Righteous Teachers, Brand Nubian, X Clan, Isis, Lakim Shabazz, KRS-One, King Sun, and Ice Cube are all promoters of the Nation of Islam's Afrocentric dogmas. Other rappers, like L. L. Cool J and Ice-T, have been known to "drop" NOI "science" on recordings and in interviews, and even the most apolitical rappers can occasionally be heard chanting the "knowledge of self" mantra, which gives them the minimal ideology needed to remain Afrocentrically correct.

Scapegoating women, homosexuals, and Jews and using classic "master race" theory, this music draws striking parallels with Nazi Aryan fantasies. But because it comes from an officially designated oppressed minority, and—even more important—because it brings in the big bucks, the sensitive souls who run the music industry have no qualms about selling it.

Public Enemy gets credit for first bringing the NOIse to rap. During the group's 1988 British tour Professor Griff, the group's self-styled "Minister of Information," denounced black gays as race traitors, Jews as instigators of the slave trade, and Caucasians as semi-anthropoids. The British music press had a field day with these and other ravings. Back in the States, the *Village Voice*'s black music critic Greg Tate quoted Griff's more outrageous pronouncements, and Public Enemy's lead singer, Chuck D, accused Tate of being a "porch nigger" in league with the "racist blue bloods" of the British music press who started the controversy.

Not that the controversy hurt these "Prophets of Rage." The group's next release, *It Takes a Nation of Millions to Hold Us Back*, sold platinum and made Public Enemy a household name. Then in May 1989, Griff, in an interview with a correspondent from the *Washington Times*, accused Jews of being responsible for "the majority of wickedness that goes on across the globe." As an authority, Griff cited a book sponsored by Henry Ford in the 1920s, *The International Jew*, which Adolf Hitler also had found of interest. The interview catapulted Public Enemy out of the insular music press and into the glare of the major media. The group came under fire from many quarters, particularly from Jewish groups. Even music industry representatives, including some from CBS, distributor of Public Enemy's Def Jam label, demanded that Griff be bumrushed from the group. Professor Griff remained defiant, daring the Jews to "send their little faggot hit men" after him.

Eventually, Chuck D reluctantly expelled Griff from Public Enemy, not because he disavowed Griff's notions, but because Griff had become a liability. Afterward, he and Griff met with NOI leader Louis Farrakhan, who reportedly scolded Griff for flaunting confidential NOI teachings before the white devil's media.

This was the most underplayed, yet most significant, event of the entire drama. It was assumed by many that Griff's rants were only his own eccentric opinions. But Griff may have functioned as more of an official NOI propagandist than anyone suspected. All his offensive remarks were taken directly from official NOI teachings, and NOI propaganda was not expelled along with Griff. If anything, Public Enemy's identification with the NOI intensified, as the cover to *Fear of a Black Planet* attests. On that record, Griff was replaced by an even more strident black supremacist, Sister Souljah.

After Malcolm X's forced resignation from the Nation of Islam and his subsequent assassination by NOI soldiers, the Nation went into an eclipse until leader Elijah Muhammad's death in 1975. The NOI then split into two factions: one led by one of Muhammad's sons, who has steered it toward mainstream Islam; the other, claiming the NOI name, led by Louis Farrakhan. The most bizarre splinter group to emerge from the NOI's factional infighting, and the one that has most influenced rappers, however, is the Five Per Cent Nation, formed by Clarence 13X after his expulsion from Malcolm X's own NOI offshoot.

The Five Per Cent Nation derives its name from an NOI teaching that 85 percent of American blacks are mentally dead as to their true nature and heritage, that 10 percent are privileged Uncle Toms who deceive the 85 percent for their white masters, and that the remaining 5 percent make up the poor righteous teachers who, knowing the truth, must instruct their benighted brethren in order to build the nation. Five Per Centers reject the NOI's stringent moral and sartorial codes, except for the prohibition of pork. As Lord Jamar of Brand Nubian figures it, "In the Five Per Cent Nation, each man is the sole controller of his own universe. If you're the God of your universe, you set up your own laws." Since Clarence 13X's death in 1969, the Five Per Centers have been leaderless, but any gods (and they commonly refer to themselves as such) who have felt the need for a chief deity have looked to Louis Farrakhan. On Brand Nubian's *In God We Trust* (1992), Farrakhan is sampled discoursing on the core similarity of NOI and Five Per Cent teachings. (Rap artists often "sample" previously recorded speeches and music by incorporating short bits of the recordings into new songs.) The Five Per Cent teachings were supposedly written by Fard Muhammad in the 1930s, but most are transmitted orally, making rap the perfect propaganda vehicle for disseminating them.

Brand Nubian is the bridge between Five Per Cent and gangsta rap. Its members wrap their amorality in the cloak of religious righteousness. They envision and agitate for a future race war that will drown the white devils in their own blood, leaving their civilization stomped "like the Stars and Stripes/burnt up in the mud." In cuts like "PasstheGat," they fantasize about robbing a gun store of its stock in order to supply their guerrilla army and killing all the (white) hostages so as not to leave any witnesses. They also would like to "shoot a faggot in the back/for acting like that."

Brand Nubian waxes arrogant in its misogyny, although one waits in vain for radical feminists such as Andrea Dworkin to call for their heads—or some more appropriate organ. "I ain't down for a honey who don't submit," intones Lord Jamar in "Love Me or Leave Me Alone." In "Steal Ya 'Ho," Jamar and Sadat X warn jealous boyfriends to keep their tempers when the Nubians steal their " 'ho," unless they want to end up in "a place with nice, soft soil." Women seem to fall into two distinct categories in the Nubians' view: either sluts or "earths," a word describing nice, Afrocentrically correct girls who are fit to bear the gods' children and help build the nation.

Poor Righteous Teachers, the other advance guards of Five Per Centism in rap, don't like "ugly"—meaning white people—any more than Brand Nubian does. More than once on their 1991 release, *Pure Poverty*, the Teachers insist that they aren't equal to "Caucasian mountain devils" or "cavemen." They are less condescending toward (black) women than Brand Nubian but are even more self-absorbed, punctuating almost every cut with their team chant, "P-R-T!" Almost all their raps on this album are Five Per Cent tirades. A *Spin* reviewer compared the lyrics to "the separatist rantings of the KKK" and recommended it to white listeners as a soundtrack to "dance your way to the gas chamber." This reviewer, unlike most of rap's white rock critic apologists, at least made the Nazi connection, although this didn't stop him from recommending the album.

Then there's Ice Cube, who declared his affinity with the Nation of Islam on his 1991 platinum release, *Death Certificate*, which showed the Cube in a morgue with a shrouded white body whose toe tag read, "Uncle Sam." On that release, Cube raged against whites, gays, Jews, Japanese, and Koreans (and the latter two he seemed to have trouble telling apart). "Who are whites and Jews to be equal to?" he growled at his fellow rappers in NWA (Niggas with Attitude, the group he began his career with), who had sinned by moving to rich white neighborhoods and letting a Jew manage their careers. "True niggers aren't gay," he snarls, while the thought of a black woman in the arms of a white man drives him into a murderous tirade.

Cube has gone Hollywood. Most recently, he had a role in John Singleton's *Higher Learning*, a movie about diversity clashes on campus. The film portrays only whites as violent racists while giving a sympathetic role to the only certifiable racist in the cast, Ice Cube himself. Predictably, the Cube always denies being a racist or an anti-Semite, insisting that he's only (guess what?) "pro-black."

Rappers influenced by the Nation of Islam have often been lauded for "educating" black youth to counter the demoralizing effects of white brainwashing and to instill pride in their African heritage. In fact, NOI/Five Per Cent rappers do not educate; they disinform. This disinformation is so radically chic that even white rappers such as Serch, formerly of 3rd Bass, endorse it: "They [blacks] are the master race, the first born. If you have a tape, like a master tape, you have one master and all the rest are copies. You have to have one point from which all others are broken down from. The original man is the black man. Period. End of conversation. There's no way you can prove it wrong."

Serch, a Jew, repeating black racists' lunatic rapping about a master race? Only in America!

Lord Jamar asks rhetorically why the Five Per Centers are the only ones able to capture black youths' attention. The question deserves an answer. The allure of Five Per Cent's mystical nihilism to an angry, pessimistic ghetto kid is obvious: If the black man is God, then, in the infamous aphorism of Hassan i Sabah (leader of the medieval Persian Assassin sect, which has some odd correspondences with Five Per Centism), "Nothing is forbidden, everything is permitted." And apparently, everything is permitted to those who disseminate the racism of the Nation of Islam and the Five Per Cent Nation through rap music, including a safe-conduct pass from rock and "progressive" media for the very crimes that are, according to current leftist dogma, the exclusive prerogatives of white males: racism, sexism, and homophobia. (No one spits out the word *faggot* as an insult as venomously or as often as these Five Per Cent rappers do.)

So where are the political correctness police when you really need them? Probably listening to this very music at their meticulously diverse soirees, all the better to express their solidarity with the black struggle. But the Nation of Islam and the Five Per Cent Nation are not "progressive" organizations. Like the Nazis, they reject scientific logic in favor of irrational pseudoscience. And, as the Klan did with Christianity, they extract the negative aspects of Islam to validate their hate and toss the rest away.

Because of their righteous negritude, they are allowed a wide latitude of political incorrectness by the Left. But greedy music-industry heads will continue to sign these hate-rappers and promote their product as long as it sells. Hypocrites like Dave Marsh and other arbiters of musical correctness will continue to whitewash black racism, pretending to deplore the hate messages while exonerating the haters and praising their efforts to "raise consciousness." Music magazines will continue to publish fawning interviews with black extremists adjacent to ads for their latest releases. And the music merchants in both the inner city and the suburban mall will continue to rake in the cash.

Government Subsidies for the Nation of Islam

Black Muslim Leonard Muhammad, accompanied by a dozen of his well-groomed, swank-suited security guards, did not come to the Cannon Office Building on March 3, 1994, to bring New York congressman Peter King one of the Nation of Islam's famous bean pies. He did not come to share his faith in Allah or the wit and wisdom of the Nation of Islam's Minister Louis Farrakhan. Muhammad, chief of staff for the Nation, was there, as Congressman King's press secretary Dan Michaelis says, to practice a little intimidation.

Two of Muhammad's imposing, red-bow-tied heavies positioned themselves at the doors of the congressman's office hallway for "safety purposes." The ten remaining practorian guards hovered ominously around their leader. Muhammad announced he was on a fact-finding mission to discover how many blacks King had on his staff. But everyone there knew that the real reason Leonard Muhammad had come calling was to make a show of power to the one man who threatens to end federal subsidies to the Nation of Islam (NOI) and Muhammad's security forces.

Over the past few years, King has been waging a nearly single-handed crusade to cut government sponsorship of NOI security programs. According to Department of Housing and Urban Development (HUD) documents, NOI's paramilitary security firms have received more than $20 million in government contracts to patrol public housing projects.

NOI security contracts began in 1989, when the Fruit of Islam—young black Muslims who function as a sort of imperial guard for Louis Farrakhan and other Muslim leaders—parlayed their voluntary patrols of Washington, D.C.'s, Mayfair Mansion and Paradise Manor apartments low-income assisted housing into a contract to do for pay what they had been doing previously for "charity." The ranks of the Fruits of Islam eventually became the recruiting ground for Nation of Islam Security, Inc. And soon the guard duty had spread from Washington, D.C., to other cities around the country.

The day before Leonard Muhammad's surprise visit to King's office, in fact, the Subcommittee on Banking and Financial Services held five and a half hours of hearings on the connection between the government and the Nation of Islam, questions of improper contracting procedures and HUD oversight of federal funds. The hearings were an embarrassment to Muhammad and his fellow NOI security force representatives because Congressman King and his fellow Republicans brought to light NOI's fraud, incompetence, brutality, and contempt for law in patrolling public housing projects, as well as the federal government's apparent lack of concern about tax dollars being used to finance an empire that supports black racism.

King began his investigation after receiving an anonymous tip in early 1994 from a HUD official. According to King, it was fairly simple. The official explained that HUD grants were going to Nation of Islam security forces and said, "You may want to look into this." The official was probably prompted to come forward by the notorious speech given by the Nation of Islam's Khalid Abdul Muhammad at Kean College in New Jersey in which Muhammad called Jews the "bloodsuckers of the black community." The speech was so stridently racist that it was condemned by both the House and the Senate in an unprecedented expression of disapproval. Despite this sentiment, however, King could not get the then Democrat-controlled House to confront the issue of significant HUD subsidies to the NOI.

The Department of Housing and Urban Development currently has nine contracts with NOI security firms in Los Angeles, Pittsburgh, Baltimore, Washington, D.C., and New York. The three main contracts are with Nation of Islam Security, Inc., in Washington, D.C., and Baltimore; with New Life Self Development, Inc., of Chicago; and with X-Men Security of New York. With the Democrats in power, this empire was secure. But the NOI got a rude awakening when Republicans stormed and captured Capitol Hill in November 1994. After more than a year of resistance from HUD, the Department of Labor, and the Department of Justice, Peter King would finally be able to get some answers.

King's hearing produced some of the most riveting congressional testimony in recent memory. Although not on King's subcommittee, Democratic Congresswoman Maxine Waters of California attended to denounce the inquiries as a "witch hunt." NOI Security Chief Abdul Sharriff Muhammad declared that the hearing was an "irrational, unreasoned, and unprincipled attack" on the Nation. And Leonard Muhammad not only refused to answer several questions posed by committee members but also accused King of being allied with the Jewish Anti-Defamation League. Nonetheless, the proceedings showed how snugly HUD was in bed with the various security firms associated with the Nation of Islam.

HUD Secretary Henry Cisneros first tried lamely to explain away any contractual relationship with NOI by saying that it was "local public housing authorities and local private housing providers, not HUD, who do the contracting for services such as security." Cisneros justified these claims by pointing to HUD's policy of making available Drug Elimination Block Grant money for local housing authorities to dispense however they choose. Then Cisneros went further in his defense of NOI: "The security firms we have identified are separate, legally incorporated entities distinct from the Nation of Islam. Even if there is an affiliation between the security firms and the Nation, thousands of local housing providers throughout the country obtain services and conduct some form of secularly related business with various organizations that have some affiliation to religious groups, such as B'nai B'rith, Habitat for Humanity, Catholic Charities, Lutheran Social Services, United Church Homes, the Salvation Army, and the establishment clause of the Constitution does not forbid such activity."

(In an editorial in response to the hearings, the *Washington Jewish Week* wrote, "The Nation of Islam, Mr. Secretary, is not analogous to B'nai B'rith or Catholic Charities—whose spokesmen do not scapegoat other minorities in sometimes blood-curdling language—but to groups like the Ku Klux Klan or neo-Nazi skinheads. NOI succeeds in controlling street crime in public housing? So did the Communist Party in Moscow.")

After months of delay and in defiance of numerous letters from Congressman King, HUD finally began a "review" of the Nation of Islam security programs. The threat of the new Republican majority and HUD's perception of vulnerability apparently made the agency willing to begin to pursue the ethical questions about NOI.

During the hearings, Assistant Secretary Roberta Achtenberg took pains to point out that HUD officials interviewed 1,000 people living at various sites protected by NOI. Cisneros and Achtenberg were proud to report that there were no significant complaints. But *Heterodoxy* magazine discovered that the survey conducted by Fair Housing and Equal Opportunity only "reviewed" the questions of discrimination against tenants by NOI officials, ignoring a host of other ethical questions.

Meyer Eisenberg, national vice-chair of the Anti-Defamation League, says, "[T]he report brushes off charges of proselytization in the housing areas, saying that those involved only isolated incidents. HUD did not investigate very thoroughly the NOI affiliates, counseling programs, and the content of its outreach and so-called 'manhood' programs." In a farcical moment, Cisneros admitted the survey had problems: "HUD staff were not able to conduct on-site interviews with [Chicago public housing] residents due to safety considerations." What he was saying, in effect, was that HUD staffers were forced to conduct interviews by phone because they were afraid to enter areas being protected by the Muslims.

According to independent inquiries, the HUD survey was not just incomplete—it was wrong. There is evidence that NOI guards often resort to violent and extreme methods. In Dallas recently, four NOI mall guards used canes and belts to beat four boys accused of shoplifting. But by far the most serious complaints have come from Chicago. At Rockwell Gardens in Chicago, the residents are much more negative about Muslim guards than was any person that HUD could produce. "There is no safety in this building now," said Francine Lomax, twenty-six, a mother of six and a six-year resident of the Chicago public housing project. "I very seldom even see the guards, so I don't let my kids out of the apartment. I don't let them play on the walkways; they don't ride their bikes."

Following a gang battle from which Muslim guards were absent, Chicago Housing Authority staffers uncovered complaints that the guards were more prone to hassle the janitorial staff than take action against the gangs that infest the buildings. CHA also found in ensuing months that New Life was not even providing the two guards stipulated in its contracts. At times there were no guards on duty at all. There is also evidence that the NOI security companies do not follow local licensing requirements, conduct background checks, or adhere to laws governing security officers.

Numerous New Life guards are felons recently out of jail after serving time for heroin or cocaine possession or robbery. A *Chicago Tribune* background check showed that of thirty guards, ten had recent felony convictions. And in Washington, D.C., Nation of Islam Security, Inc., lost a contract because two security guards kicked a police officer in the face and stole his gun. NOI security company representatives maintain that what they do is incredible. "We are in very dangerous communities unarmed. We don't come there seeking to intimidate our people; we come there seeking to raise their level of consciousness and prove to them that they themselves can improve and be reformed," says Leonard Muhammad.

But in reality, the alleged ability of these unarmed prophets to prevent crime is largely fictional. The *Chicago Tribune* reported that "some current and former guards said New Life [Muslim security company] supervisors discouraged them from writing reports about violent incidents in the project—potentially suppressing statistics and making Rockwell [housing project] look safer than it is."

As his investigation progressed, Congressman King found ample evidence of the politically correct double standard: "HUD asks for the records. Nation of Islam says it doesn't have them. HUD then says it doesn't have the power to enforce it. If it was an ordinary contractor they would have found a way."

King's aide Dan Michaelis adds, "I cannot imagine another federally funded contract would be allowed to proceed with the oversight being so lax. Any other federal contract you have to make sure you have all the 'i's dotted and the 't's crossed."

There is also evidence suggesting that NOI firms have highly questionable hiring practices. In the Baltimore area, approximately 20 percent of the security guards for projects are white. But there are no whites on the NOI security forces roster. Leonard Muhammad told Congress that there has been only one white applicant, and he wasn't qualified.

Normally an entire workforce of one race and one sex would send up red flags to the Department of Labor, whose regulations prohibit discrimination among federal contractors. But here too NOI gets a free ride. In addition, the subcommittee hearings discovered that

NOI security firms have refused to file employment data with the Equal Employment Opportunity Commission. The EEOC, despite several letters from HUD officials and King himself, has not followed up on the matter.

Are the security firms tied into Farrakhan's bigger empire? Defenders of the relationship between HUD and NOI deny that this is the case. But, in fact, according to one of the brochures that is distributed by on-duty X-men guards on Coney Island, to "take away the security contract would destroy the financial base of the Nation of Islam."

The relationship is symbiotic, according to *The Final Call*, the Nation of Islam's official newspaper. Dion Muhammad, vice president and executive director of the Nation of Islam Security, was quoted in August 1994 on the connection: "The growth and success of the company is based on the guidance of the Honorable Louis Farrakhan, the discipline of the Nation of Islam, and the direction of Security Chief Abdul Sharriff Muhammad."

The Final Call also notes that Fruit of Islam members are equal in rank to and interchangeable with Nation of Islam Security, Inc., guards and the guards from other NOI security companies.

In a 1992 interview, NOI's supreme captain, William Muhammad, advocated that proceeds from NOI security firms go to Farrakhan. Then he explained why NOI security teams were being criticized in the media: "Some people, particularly some Jews, don't want any financial benefits to come to Minister Farrakhan. They tell this lie that the minister hates Jews and that we are anti-Semitic. That's a cover to keep us from establishing an economic base."

But NOI security firms do more than move government funds to Farrakhan. William Muhammad explains the place of this dark star in the NOI's twisted firmament. He says, "NOI security is a holistic program; we don't just deal with security. The important program is our social program."

NOI preaches self-reliance, cleanliness, punctuality, self-respect, and hard work. But NOI's hate-filled rhetoric, while attractive to young blacks hungry for empowerment, is corrosive and ultimately dangerous, as the NOI "manhood" programs clearly show. The manhood programs are a mélange of psychotherapy and paramilitary training. Those attending the programs are indoctrinated with NOI dogma and "theology" as well as with military exercises conducted to the chants of Islamic holy men.

On June 8, 1994, HUD Secretary Henry Cisneros met with King. According to Michaelis, the meeting was a success: "It was a 180-degree [turn] from Secretary Cisneros as far as his willingness to cooperate and perform a real investigation. We managed to pass the stonewalling stage. It's reason for some encouragement."

As a result of the meeting, Cisneros agreed to begin more serious investigations of federal support for the Nation of Islam. Would it have taken this long if the money had been flowing to the Ku Klux Klan or some other equally racist organization?

When Louis Met Tom

Give Louis Farrakhan five minutes and he'll introduce you to his enemies. "Practically everywhere I have gone, the Jews have gone in front of me stirring people against me," the Nation of Islam leader wrote in the organization's newspaper, *The Final Call*, on May 9, 1988. "Listen, Jews," *New York* magazine reports that he said on October 7, 1985, "you cannot say 'never again' to God, because when He puts you in the oven, 'never again' don't mean a thing." And, as the *New York Post* revealed on May 23, 1988, Farrakhan declared in Flushing, New York, "The Jews cannot defeat me. I will grind them and crush them into little bits."

Louis Farrakhan should be judged not just by those he calls his foes but, more important, by his friends. Farrakhan fails this test too. Amazingly, Farrakhan and the Nation of Islam have accepted money from and cooperated with members of white supremacy groups, including veterans of the Ku Klux Klan.

"I was a guest of Louis Farrakhan's organization in Los Angeles," Tom Metzger told me by telephone in the summer of 1993, confirming reports published in the *Washington Times* and the *Washington Post* in the fall of 1985. Metzger, the former Grand Dragon of the California KKK and the current head of the White Aryan Resistance, attended a Farrakhan rally at the Fabulous Forum on September 14, 1985, along with a half dozen of his racist cronies.

"It's not true," Leonard Muhammad, Farrakhan's chief of staff, says of Metzger's story. "Our meetings are open to [whom]ever wants to come." Yet Metzger insists that he and his associates were invited to the affair by Farrakhan's staff. "I'm sure it had his authorization," Metzger explains. "They roped off a small section toward the back of the auditorium just for us."

"We were treated quite well," Metzger recalls. He notes that he and his guests gave $100 to Farrakhan and the Nation of Islam organization as a "gesture of understanding." He adds that the contribution was acknowledged by the on-stage announcer. Asked about this donation, Muhammad replied, "I have no comment on that."

Farrakhan apparently impressed Metzger. "I like what I hear," Metzger said in the September 30, 1985, *Washington Times*. "They speak out against the Jews and the oppressors in Washington," he added. "Louis Farrakhan is an honest black man who is not embarrassed or ashamed to stand up and say what he feels."

Metzger's fondness for Farrakhan is more than just a schoolboy crush. A convergence of interest unites white supremacists and the Nation of Islam. "They want their own territory and that's exactly what we want for them and for ourselves," Metzger has said. They share a "concern about the survival of two separate and distinct races," Metzger said, later adding, "They are the black counterpart of us."

Hold up a mirror to Metzger's remarks and you will see the words Farrakhan uttered on March 11, 1984, which appeared in *Insight* magazine on November 11, 1985: "Some white people are going to live . . . but [God] don't want them living with us. He doesn't want us mixing ourselves up with the slavemaster's children, whose time of doom has arrived."

Farrakhan threatened that if presidential aspirant Jesse Jackson were denied a role in the 1984 Democratic convention, Farrakhan would "lead an army of black men and women to Washington, D.C., and negotiate . . . for a separate state or territory of our own."

Tom Metzger also remembers the Jackson campaign. He says he "gave the Nation of Islam information about the movement of Jewish extremists we thought might be a threat to Jackson." No fan of Jackson, Metzger wanted to keep white separatists from being blamed for attacks he says they did not make.

Metzger also told me, "The Anti-Defamation League was under fire in San Francisco for collecting files on people. A stack of files [on the Nation of Islam] came into my hands. I called the Nation of Islam. They came to my home, and I turned the files over to them as a goodwill gesture."

Farrakhan's obsession with Jews unites him with other white extremists. At the October 1985 Christian Patriots Annual Conference in Michigan, Chicago-area white supremacist Art Jones told a gathering of 200 cross-burning, Nazi-uniform-clad racists: "The enemy of my enemy is my friend. I salute Louis Farrakhan and anyone else who stands up against the Jews."

Farrakhan and Metzger are birds of a feather. Their flights of paranoia have led them along separate but equal paths to the same hate-filled fantasy land. It's important to add that this sad symbiosis between Farrakhan and white bigots should not diminish the valuable work of many NOI members who peacefully call for self-reliance, strong families, and an ethical renaissance among black Americans.

Like him or not, Farrakhan does have the constitutionally protected right to spew 150-proof anti-Semitic venom at the disturbingly large crowds that gather before him. Perhaps someone will use that same right to ask Farrakhan a very simple question: How can a man in cahoots with cross-burners call himself a black leader?

Afrocentric Curriculum

R a-hotep positioned himself in the cockpit as a dozen of his brawniest workers drew back on the catapult. They released the lever, and the wood-and-papyrus glider was flung forward into the sky. The sleek, cunningly designed craft, with its reverse dihedral wing configuration, quickly caught the hot updrafts from the Egyptian desert and slipped the surly bonds of earth, wafting high into the cloudless sky in ever widening circles. Soaring up over the new pyramid construction at Cheops, Ra-hotep turned north to follow the Nile's liquid swath, the life-giving stream that irrigated crops as far as the eye could see. He marveled at the wonders his dark-skinned people had created. On this very day, after landing the glider, he would join his uncle, Ta-minsheshak, at his estate near the holy city of Raminafu, where a contingent of Greeks was due to arrive from Europe for their regular lessons in philosophy, literature, and mathematics. The Greeks were a pale, crude, and primitive people, whose knowledge remained in a rudimentary state. But they came in peace, and Ra-hotep saw in them a desire to learn and expand their wisdom. Today, he would personally teach them how comets had created the Nile and the oceans. He would lead them into the mysteries of magical precognition and psychokinesis. Below he saw the signal for the landing strip, and Ra-hotep began his slow descent to the earth. . . .

Absurd though it sounds, in the hands of an eager and creative instructor, this scenario could easily be extracted from a widely used set of educational curricula, the African American Baseline Essays, produced by the Portland Public Schools, and be integrated into almost any classroom in America. The science section of these essays says that from 2500 B.C. to 1500 B.C. the "Egyptians used their early planes for travel, expeditions, and recreation" and concludes with a vision of African people as being "the wellspring of creativity and knowledge on which the foundation of all science, technology and engineering rests." The Portland Baseline Essays are the most widely used of all Afrocentric teacher resources. Craig Kurath of the Portland School District says that sales (the essays cost $12 to produce and carry a price of $25) have been "very hot" and that thousands of the resource packets have been sold to districts and individual educators in Denver, Chicago, Kansas City, Atlanta, Detroit, Cleveland, Seattle, Indianapolis, Los Angeles, and other cities. Carolyn Leonard, Portland's coordinator of multicultural education, reports that there has been keen interest in the essays at teacher conferences. There are hundreds of back orders, and some bookstores carry the essays, which have also been sold to Australia, Japan, and Britain. Kurath reports that school districts in the Virgin Islands recently ordered 100 copies.

The Portland Baseline Essays have been in circulation since 1987, but although they have grown steadily more influential within the educational establishment, little has been written about them. It is easy to see why mum has been the word, for the development and dissemination of these essays provide a textbook study in minority power politics, intellectual quackery, bureaucratic acquiescence, and journalistic deference to political correctness.

Though far from the Jim Crow South in both distance and customs, the Portland School District, the largest in the Pacific Northwest, was under fire in the late 1970s to follow a court-ordered desegregation plan. One of the key pressure groups clashing with the schools was the Black United Front. "When they decide they want change, they get it," Carolyn Leonard says of the activist group. "They don't negotiate." The Baseline Essays confirm that the Front wanted radical Afrocentrism from the schools and got it. (These essays, it is stated in the preface, are "a direct result of the interaction of the Black United Front and the Desegregation Monitoring Advisory Committee with the Portland School District.") The Desegregation Monitoring Advisory Committee duly reviewed the material, along with the Multicultural/Multiethnic Educational Task Force and the African American Curriculum Consultants.

But even though they emerged from Portland's highly sensitized racial politics, the essays were not a local project. The concept was introduced to Portland Public Schools in 1981 by Dr. Asa G. Hilliard, a member of the Association of Black Psychologists and "the primary consultant" to the project. The choice of Hilliard for this role was a significant one. In an essay on Afrocentrism written for the July/August 1995 issue of the Library of Congress magazine, *Civilization*, Gerald Early, director of Afro-American studies at Washington University in St. Louis, notes that "Afrocentrism is related to the rise of 'black psychology' as a discipline." The Association of Black Psychologists, organized during the radical heyday of 1968, argued that to repair a collectively damaged black psyche, it would be necessary to destroy "Eurocentrism" and its "white values" of "rationality, order, and individualism." The Association of Black Psychologists, says Early, charged that such values were "totally inimical to the political and psychological interests of black people."

Carol Innerst, an education writer who has attended conferences on Afrocentric education, reports that Professor Hilliard (who teaches at Georgia State University) is not exactly affable to those less than worshipful of his curricula. She notes that the prime movers of Afrocentrism were the National Black United Front, the National Urban Coalition, the National Alliance of Black Educators, and the Association for the Study of Classical African Civilization.

Key figures, besides Hilliard, include such noted Afrocentrist professors as melanin-theorist Leonard Jeffries of the City College of New York and Conrad Worrill of Northeastern Illinois University in Chicago. The "target cities" for the dissemination of their materials are St. Louis, Kansas City, New York, Chicago, Seattle, Atlanta, and Washington, D.C. The Portland Baseline Essays were a godsend to this group.

The African American Baseline Essays comprise five sections (art, science and technology, language arts, mathematics, and music), each of which, says the preface, "has been authored by an individual who is both knowledgeable about the specific discipline and recognized as an expert on African and African-American History." Dr. John Beerworth, Portland's current superintendent of education, declines to say whether he believed the essays present students with the most accurate information from the best available scholars. But Lou Frederick, director of public information for the district, says that "four people went line by line through the essays" to ensure accuracy. Judging from what has been left in, the reader can only wonder what materials were considered questionable enough to take out.

"Egypt was a Black African Society," says Michael Harris of Morehouse College in Atlanta, author of the art section, who believes that "Egyptian culture had its developmental origins further south in the African interior." And since Egypt was a black nation, "the art forms and architecture we relate to Egypt are in fact, forms of Black art." The force of this black civilization "propelled the culture for 3,000 years, changed the cultures of the conquering Greeks and Romans, and provided the foundation for the world's science, mathematics, and religion. Only the destructive forces of Christianity from Rome, and the sweep of Islam were able to stop the living practice of the Egyptian Mysteries." Reed College graduate Joyce Braden Harris, cofounder of Portland's Black Educational Center, writes in the language arts essay, "Non-Africans were not responsible for Egypt's greatness, Black Africa was, since the two

were one and the same during Egypt's most productive periods."
Harris's list of African authors includes Pushkin, Alexandre Dumas,
and Aesop, whose name, she argues, "was derived from the Greek
word Ethiop, which meant sunburned face." In addition to subtract-
ing these famous writers from the white world and adding them to
the company of Beethoven as honorary blacks, Harris writes about
the contemporary literary scene: "Black literature is manipulated
and controlled by white editors and publishers. . . . Black writers
who are published generally receive little or no promotion for their
works. Poor sales are then cited as reasons for not accepting
manuscripts from Black authors and putting the works that are
published out of print." She does not indicate how this squares with
celebrity achieved by talented black writers like Toni Morrison and
less talented ones like Alice Walker. But she does recommend *Selec-
tions from the Usia*, by Ron Karenga, who "has done a superb job of
translating Egyptian literature into everyday language." (During the
1960s, Karenga, now a California State University at Long Beach
professor, was part of U.S.—"United Slaves"—a violent cultural
nationalist group whose bloody turf wars with the Black Panthers
culminated in a shoot-out in a UCLA cafeteria.)

In the mathematics essay, Beatrice Lumpkin, retired professor of
math at Malcolm X College in Chicago, writes that "the historians
[could not] admit that Black people had built this great civilization
because to do so would contradict the theories of racial inferiority
used as a cover for slavery and colonialism. And so they invented the
theory of 'white' Egyptians who were merely browned by the sun."
She adds that "since Africa is widely believed to be the birthplace of
the human race, it follows that Africa was the birthplace of mathematics and science." Thus does Lumpkin reveal the non sequitur
reasoning on which Afrocentrism is based.

John Henrik Clarke, professor emeritus of African World History
at Hunter College and author of the social studies essay, says, "The
Europeans not only colonized most of the world, but also began to

colonize information about the world and its people. In order to do this, they had to forget, or pretend to forget, all they had previously known about the Africans." Professor Clarke's historical-religious observations include the following: "There are misconceptions about the role the Hebrews played in Africa. . . . They came originally from Western Asia, escaping famine. They literally entered world history during this period and were treated much better in Africa than history tends to indicate. Non-biblical history of the period indicates the Hebrews were not slaves in Egypt. Some of the Hebrews mistakenly took sides with the enemies of Africa and were punished. . . . The Hebrews, like the Greeks, Romans, Hyksos, and other foreigners, benefited religiously and intellectually from their sojourn in Africa. What they learned there would influence all of their future history."

Professor Clarke also asserts that Cleopatra was part Greek and part African and that if she were alive today, "she would probably be living in one of the Black communities of the United States."

Charshee Lawrence-McIntyre, of the State University of New York, Old Westbury, one of the authors billed as knowledgeable about her discipline, contributed the essay on music, which reads like a combination of a high school music text and rejected reviews from *Downbeat*. She refers to the late Chet Baker, a well-known and respected white jazz trumpet player, as a guitarist, which is roughly equivalent to describing Jerry Garcia as a zither virtuoso. In addition to this howler, the author joins the other essayists in asserting that it is from Africa that all good things flow. "The basics of music in the Western world both European and African-American can be traced to Africa (particularly Egypt)," Lawrence-McIntyre writes. She goes on to give a new twist to the old notion that blacks "have rhythm" by saying that drummer Meade Lux Lewis "managed to keep two rhythms going at once—something any African drummer does automatically, based on the phenomenon of the African sense of rhythm." Unfortunately, Meade Lux Lewis was a piano player.

But of all the pieces in the Baseline Essays, by far the most interesting is the one on science and technology. The author, Hunter Havelin Adams III, believes that "science is the search for unity and wholeness within the totality of human experience." He quotes from Ruth Bleier's *Feminist Approaches to Science*: "The dominant categories of cultural experience—race, gender, religion, and class—will be reflected in the cultural institution of science itself; in its structure, theories, concepts, values, ideologies and practices." In this view, science becomes another clever trick of oppressive white males to keep blacks and women down. Yet Adams also believes that all people "not only are scientists, but, at a more fundamental level, science itself." Within this democracy of talent, however, the Egyptians were more equal than others. "Training to be a priest/scientist in Egypt was a long, arduous process," Adams writes. And: "The earth today, and for hundreds of millions of years, has been inundated by water-laden micro-comets, which not only over time were the source of the ocean's water, but of rivers' water like the Nile."

The ancient Egyptians, who of course were black Africans, were "masters of magic precognition, psychokinesis, remote viewing and other underdeveloped human capabilities," Adams claims. And who could forget the fact that thousands of years before the Wright brothers, there were the gliders?

One design found in a tomb "looks contemporary and bears a strong resemblance to the American Hercules transport aircraft which has a distinctive reverse dihedral wing." But this was only the scale model of actual early planes that the Egyptians used for "travel, expeditions, and recreation."

The Baseline Essays identify Hunter Havelin Adams III as a "Research Scientist, Historian and Consultant" at the Department of Energy's Argonne National Laboratory near Chicago. But the line-by-line fact checkers who, according to Portland school officials, went over this publication with a fine-tooth comb apparently failed to verify these qualifications. Adams's former boss at the Argonne Lab confirms that Adams did indeed work there from 1970 to 1991, but not as a research scientist. He was an "industrial hygiene consultant," a position requiring no college degree or scientific training.

Staff in the Portland School District say they don't know where Adams is or what he is doing. Carl Spight, who reviewed the science essay and holds a Ph.D. in Astrophysical Science from Princeton, did not return calls for this article. (Both Spight and Adams are listed as founders of something called the Life-Ways Sciences Institute.) Another reviewer of Adams's material was Kamau Anderson, also known as Kamau Sadiki. He did not return calls either.

With so many legitimate African American scholars to choose from, one must wonder how Adams the hygiene consultant was selected to write a science essay that is now used across the United States and abroad. The choice, it seems, was one not of qualifications but of politics. "Asa Hilliard recommended the people," says Portland's Carolyn Leonard, adding that the Black United Front also supported the choices. Leonard says she had serious doubts about some of the authors and their material, but no dissent was allowed by the Black United Front. "If you raise a question, you are challenged," she says, recalling one meeting where a single adverse comment "made the meeting fall apart."

For these hard-core Afrocentrists, Adams's lack of qualifications is actually an advantage. Gerald Early writes in *Civilization* that *Stolen Legacy* and other key Afrocentric texts were "not written by professional historians or by college professors." The fact that several classic Afrocentric texts have been written by amateurs, he says, "gives Afrocentrism its powerful populist appeal, its legitimacy as an expression of 'truth' that white institutional forces hide or obscure. At the same time, this leaves it vulnerable to charges of being homemade, unprofessional, theoretically immature and the like. . . . [Nonetheless] it has developed a cadre of academics to speak for it, to professionalize it, to make it a considerable insurgency movement on the college campus."

And for some Afrocentrists, the real test of the material is what whites think of it. Carolyn Leonard says that the response of some black activists in Portland was that "if white people like them, there must be something wrong." But a number of scholars and intellectuals, black and white, see plenty wrong with Afrocentrism in general and the Portland Baseline Essays in particular. "It's a pathetic fantasy . . . silly, hokey, revisionist pseudo-science," says Shelby Steele, "a compensatory grandiosity for this feeling of defeat and shame at having been victimized and enslaved and pushed to the perimeter." Steele, author of *The Content of Our Character*, adds, "when you deal in this sort of blarney the true contributions get overlooked. What nobody wants to say is that this is just bone ignorance, backed up by thuggishness and collaborated with by school systems and universities across the country. It's a humiliation to black people."

"Afrocentrism fails to transcend European categories of race, class and culture," writes Clarence Walker, history professor at the University of California, Davis, and author of *Deromanticizing Black History*. "Their tools of social analysis are Western, not African. . . . Ultimately, Afrocentrism is Eurocentrism in blackface. It repeats what it sets out to repudiate." In the same vein, Frank Yurco, an Egyptologist associated with the Field Museum of Natural History and the University of Chicago, notes that "the ancient Egyptians' lack of color prejudice should serve as another salutary lesson for us all today. It also contradicts the Afrocentric view that the ancient Egyptians called themselves and considered themselves 'black.' Anthropological and artistic evidence shows they did not."

The Portland Essays not only push a radically irrational view of Afrocentism but also take pan-Africanism to new extremes, arguing that "cultural unity is evident among African people on the continent of Africa and throughout the world." By this standard, blacks in Harlem or San Francisco's Hunter's Point have more in common culturally with Tutsis and Hutus in Rwanda than with white Americans. Rosalind Johnson, a Spanish and French teacher in Maryland, who is part black and part Indian, says that such Afrocentric curricula "promote fantasy as fact" and worries that children exposed to materials such as these "will graduate from these programs with a lousy education. They might come away thinking that the continent of Africa was and is a monolithic society, rather than a place where millions of people speak thousands of dialects and live in both conflict and harmony."

But critics of the Portland Essays will find the going rough. When the "official" and therefore "white" world challenges these pieces, it only fuels the radical Afrocentrists' belief in a white, oppressive conspiracy. Such paranoia does not surprise someone like Wilson Moses, professor of history at Pennsylvania State University and author of *The Golden Age of Black Nationalism*. Moses, who has traced efforts to link black Americans and ancient Egyptians to as far back as an 1827 newspaper editorial, says, "Afrocentrism is not an intellectual movement; it is a secular religion." He calls Afrocentrism "a born-again, true-believer type of enthusiasm, similar to creation science and rationalized with the same sort of evangelical passion. It is not likely to be stopped by intellectual arguments."

But materials such as those in the Portland Essays make some critics ready to rumble. Michael Meyers of the New York Civil Rights Coalition and a former assistant director of the NAACP writes that "the scholar's duty is to reject fakery, primitivism, and anti-intellectualism. Afrocentrism, in my view, is all three . . . scholars, students, and teachers should examine and confront all racial idiocies. If they do, they will eschew black imitations of white racism." Meyers believes that the time has come for scholars to get angry, not just upset, at Afrocentrism. "Scholars will have to take on their fellow academicians—not just in the academic journals and in their publications, but on their own campuses and on the campuses where Afrocentrists have their strongholds. We need to recognize that the marketplace of ideas requires not only debate, but debaters. We need to get busy."

But today it seems that the ones getting busy are the Afrocentrists and their allies in education. Carolyn Leonard says that the multicultural officials in Portland are aware of the criticisms of the Baseline Essays. She says she was personally shocked at some of the material in the essays, particularly the passages about gliders flying in the shadow of the pyramids. But neither the inaccuracies nor the falsification of Mr. Adams's qualifications proved objectionable enough to bump the fake Dr. Science from the approved list. According to Leonard, the new, revised African American Baseline Essays, published in September 1995, still contain material by Adams but excise his bogus credentials.

"Districts call and say they want the essays because they tried to develop their own curricula and wound up throwing up their hands," says Portland school administrator Craig Kurath. Meanwhile, the Hispanic Baseline Essays are in draft form and a collection for American Indians went to press in September 1996. Just what they will say about Indian civilization has not been revealed. One wonders if they will suggest that the Mohegans were driving prototypes of the Model T through the Adirondacks before the arrival of the Puritans.

Queen of Afrocentrism

W hen student activists at the Office of Multicultural Affairs at the University of Toledo staged a debate on *The Bell Curve*, a controversial look at IQ and race, they decided to pit Charles Murray, co-author of the work, against Dr. Frances Cress Welsing, a black psychiatrist from Washington, D.C., who is the creator of the "Cress Theory of Color Confrontation and Racism (White Supremacy)." The university's student newspaper, *The Collegian*, indicated that Welsing had "successfully countered" theories similar to Murray's in a 1974 debate with Nobel laureate Dr. William Shockley. But it was less Welsing's forensic skills that made activists invite her to Toledo than her reputation as reigning queen of Afrocentrism and one of the most influential, if little known, black radical intellectuals. While Toledo multiculturalists damned Murray's views as racist, in pitting him against Welsing they knew they were fighting fire with fire.

In their coverage of the debate, which they implied had been a draw, the Toledo press indicated that Welsing had managed to make Murray's theories seem a little bizarre. She had the advantage of being a counterpuncher in this confrontation and could concentrate on attacking her opponent. But for the purely bizarre, Frances Cress Welsing's own ideas may well be unparalleled, making even her brother in Afrocentrism, Leonard Jeffries (who shares Welsing's belief that blacks are superior to whites because they have more melanin in their skin), seem semi-respectable by comparison. Welsing's theories are presented in *The Isis Papers: The Keys to the Colors*, a collection of essays spanning 1970 to 1988 in which she developed her critique of "the global system of white supremacy (racism)," as she habitually calls it. For her, whites, and whites only, are or can be racists. From the dedication, she tries to shut up objections, stating that no white person should "presume to tell any Black person (or other non-white person) what racism is or is not." Yet the truth is that if the word *racist* cannot be applied to Welsing and other blacks who think like her, then it has become a word with no meaning at all, for *The Isis Papers* are a virtual *Mein Kampf* of Afrocentricity.

Like the Nation of Islam's theology, Welsing's theory rests on the assumption that blacks are the original members of the "hue-man" race, while whites are the mutant albino result of a relatively recent, spontaneous genetic mutation. These melanin-deficient misfits (melanin plays an important, mystical role in Welsing's thinking, as will be shown later) were then driven into exile from Africa by their disdainful, melanin-enriched parents, finding refuge in what is now Europe.

In the caves and forests of darkest Europa, the whites stagnated in savagery, according to Welsing, interbreeding until all traces of their African origin disappeared. Finally, the Greeks managed to rise far enough up out of this degeneracy to steal their civilization from the black Egyptians. Then the Romans, followed by all subsequent European powers, embarked on a genocidal conquest against those who had originally rejected and exiled them and knew the secret of their shameful origin. This anti-black genocide, Welsing maintains, peaked with the African slave trade and continues to this day.

Perhaps aware that this bizarre theory isn't going to be taken too seriously as a plausible explanation for white racism, Welsing tries to prove that the real motivation behind white racism is survival rather than revenge. She maintains that whites are genetically recessive while blacks are genetically dominant—hence, whites' frantic efforts to prevent intermarriage, especially between black men and white women, since the offspring will be technically black. (Welsing is as much a believer in the "one drop" theory of racial identity as is any Jim Crow segregationist.)

This crusade to prevent the genetically and numerically weak whites from being drowned in a flood of miscegenation, Welsing contends, explains the white power structure's genocidal wars against colored peoples and its desperate dedication to keeping the white supremacy system intact at any cost. In an effort to bring coherence to her theory (which doesn't bother to explain abolitionism, the civil rights movement, affirmative action, mandated multicultural studies, or the invitation that brought her to the University of Toledo), Welsing has concocted what she refers to as "Unified Field Theory Psychiatry," claiming to have done for Freudian psychology what Einstein sought to do for particle physics: construct a theory that explains everything, at least from the perspective of her own racial/sexual obsessions. Thus Welsing claims to have decoded the hidden racial meanings of the Christian cross and the swastika; guns, balls, and games; cigars, pipes, and cigarettes; paper money and gold; boxing; black leather and lingerie; chocolate and Valentine's Day gifts; black tuxedos and white wedding dresses; Moby Dick; Adam and Eve; sun-tanning; dogs; cowboys; and the "meaning" of rape. Coincidentally, all the hidden meanings are revealed as confirmations of Welsing's theory, exactly what she thought she would find. (AMERICA, for instance, is an anagram for I AM RACE, and guess which pigment, or lack thereof, turns out to be "the neurochemical basis for evil"?)

In her unified theory, Welsing believes, for instance, that any time whites put on black clothing (such as tuxedos, leather jackets, or black lace lingerie), they are attempting symbolically to don black skin. And any ingestion of dark foods or drinks (such as coffee or chocolate) is an attempt to regain the dark pigmentation lost in that distant African genetic mutation. Sun-tanning is an even more obvious attempt to recapture that lost melanin. Similarly, any long, dark cylindrical object, such as a cigar or a gun, is symbolic of the genitally inadequate white male's obsession with what he lacks and most desires: a big black penis. (Phallocrat that she is, a cigar is never just a cigar to Dr. Welsing.)

Here is Welsing's peculiar interpretation of the Christian cross: "I submit that the cross . . . is none other than a brain-computer distillate of the white collective's fear-induced obsession with the genitals of all non-white men (of Black men in particular), who have the potential to genetically annihilate the white race. Furthermore, the cross represents the Black male's genitals removed from the Black male's body—meaning castrated genitals. Thus, the cross is a critical symbol in the thought processes of the white supremacy system, beginning its evolution almost 2,000 years ago during early white aggression against Blacks in Africa and Asia. This particular interpretation of the cross never has been given before."

The Roman emperor Constantine I, who legalized Christianity, placed the motto *In Hoc Signo Vinces*—"In this sign you shall conquer"—on the cross, Welsing contends, to inspire whites to world domination. And the Nazi swastika, she further elucidates, is "the cross in motion," spurring whites on to a frenzy of genocide against people of color. To the possible objection that the majority of the Nazis' victims, Jews, were white and that Nazism was an ideology based on anti-Semitism, Welsing has a response: Semite does not mean a descendant of Shem, son of Noah, ancestor of modern Jews and Arabs, but "is from the Latin prefix, semi meaning 'half'—half Black and half white, and that means mulatto (non-white)."

Then what does the image of Jesus crucified on the cross signify? To Welsing, it represents two related concepts. First, it symbolizes the crucifixion/castration of black males. (Jesus was, of course, "undoubtedly a Black man," living in Africa, not Palestine, whose blood—or black genetic material—was shed to "save" the genetically recessive whites from genetic annihilation—that is, interbreeding—and confer "everlasting life" on the pure white minority.) The second concept is that of a "frail, weak, effeminate, suffering and dying white Christ . . . hung against a black wooden cross," signifying that "the weak, genetic recessive, white male will be destroyed genetically speaking, when up against the white-annihilating, genetically dominant, Black male genital apparatus (the cross)."

Without missing a beat, Welsing goes from the sublime to the ridiculous in her unified theory, from Christ to cowboys, about whom she has the following insights: "[It is] interesting . . . that the whites who raised, bred and herded brown and black cattle referred to themselves as 'cowboys,' a highly interesting word which doubly effeminizes these males. The word 'cow,' while it can be used broadly to refer to any domesticated bovine, is used most specifically to refer to the mature female cattle. Similarly, the word 'boy' historically has been used by whites in the U.S. to refer to the Black male as a means of minimizing and degrading his masculinity." In other words, the cowboy is actually a horse-riding gay man. Ignoring the fact that numerous black cowboys also helped drive cattle up the Chisholm Trail to Dodge City, she also sees white cowboys roping, branding, and castrating black and brown cattle as more symbolic lynching of black men, and the slaughter of woolly-haired buffalo as the symbolic extermination of black people. To those who would observe that the reason for all this hard, dirty work was to put meat on the tables of city dwellers, Welsing has a ready response: "Beef is the preferred meat of the majority of whites in the global white supremacy system and culture. Beef eaters are supposed to be or to become more powerful and masculine."

Welsing contends that the majority of cowboys, buffalo hunters, and gunfighters were dispossessed southerners. Humiliated by their defeat in the Civil War and by the loss of their slaves, they salvaged their masculinity by transferring their racism to herds of innocent animals, which they slaughtered, and found a powerful penis substitute in the barrel of a .44 revolver. The alleged obsession of white males with guns is one of Welsing's favorite themes: "Guns and missiles are

viewed as essential aspects of white male anatomy and physiology. Is
it an accident that in the U.S. white male children learn to use guns
before they learn to use their penises, while Black male children
learn to use their penises before they learn to use guns?"

Welsing is one of the premier white male bashers of our day,
which would automatically reserve her a place in the multicultural
pantheon were it not for her raging homophobia; but to Welsing,
one complements the other: "Historically, white males worldwide
have suffered the deep sense of male inferiority and inadequacy because they represent a mutant, genetically recessive, minority population that can be genetically annihilated by all non-white
people—male and females. Ultimately, this awareness in the white
collective has produced high levels of masculine self-doubt, fear,
anxiety, and self-alienation. These difficulties have been intensified
by the awareness that white reproductivity is far lower than the natural reproductivity of any non-white population."

This sense of inadequacy leads the white male to oppress the
white female (because at least she's inferior to him), who retaliates
by effeminizing her sons, producing homosexuals, or, as Welsing
puts it, "a female with a penis." If white females are given their total
freedom, Welsing contends, they will then "sexually aggress" against
black males, their true desired sex partners. Welsing believes this
unconscious desire is given away by the traditional romantic formula
of "tall, dark, and handsome." This is partially due to the resentful
white woman's desire to capture that which the white male most
fears and envies—a large, "powerful," black penis—and partially
because, subconsciously aware of her genetic, melanin-deficient
inferiority, her ultimate desire is to produce a baby of color.

And how did Welsing arrive at this conclusion? Because black
men who have had sex with white women have claimed that this is a
"frequent utterance" of these women. To Welsing such anecdotal
hearsay is "vivid testimony" of the scientific validity of her theory.

Actually, Welsing can't decide whether white male homosexuality is the result of the effeminizing influence of repressed

white mothers or of inherent genetic weakness. She sees this effeminacy as having been repressed throughout history as long as whites were on top, but once dark-skinned peoples began to revolt, the white male's true effeminate nature came forth with a vengeance. She even muses at one point, "Is there a relationship among the number of white males seeking sex change operations (to remove their hated male genitalia) . . . and the white male's loss of the Vietnam war to non-white men . . . ?"

Welsing will not endear herself to ACT-UP or Queer Nation with an analysis of homosexual behavior such as this: "White male homosexuality may be viewed as the symbolic attempt to incorporate into the white male body more male substance by either sucking the penis of another male and orally ingesting the semen, or by having male ejaculate deposited in the other end of the alimentary canal. Through anal intercourse, the self-debasing white male may fantasize that he can produce a product of color, albeit that the product of color is fecal matter."

But what about black homosexuality? Welsing sees this as part of the white supremacy system's conspiracy to symbolically castrate black men—as lynch mobs once physically castrated them: "Unlike the white male, the Black male does not arrive at the effeminate bisexual or homosexual stance from any deeply repressed sense of genetic weakness, inadequacy or disgust, which I refer to as primary effeminacy (effeminacy that is self-derived and not imposed forcibly by others). Instead, the Black male arrives at this position secondarily, as the result of the imposed power and cruelty of the white male . . . that has forced 20 generations of Black males into submission." Black homosexuality is victimization that blacks must "treat" to "prevent its continuing and increasing occurrence."

While Welsing seems at times to be benevolently willing to allow the white race to be slowly bred into oblivion via miscegenation and homosexuality, her true intentions surface with dire hints of a necessary global bloodbath to "neutralize this global and most monstrous form of injustice and chaos." Welsing sees this system of racism as an international conspiracy manipulated consciously by the white elite and acted upon, unconsciously for the most part, by the white masses and uniting all white people regardless of their differences. Welsing marshals the most obscure evidence in behalf of this idea. A newspaper article from 1980 on Western governments bailing out the Polish economy, for instance, suggests to her not an effort to woo a disgruntled Soviet satellite or the readiness of capitalists to do business even with their proclaimed enemies, but an example of the "global white collective" setting aside political differences to unite in a common front of white supremacy: "All white peoples have the spoken or unspoken mandate to participate actively in their collective struggle for global white genetic survival. This specifically means, of necessity, the murder and slaughter of Black and other non-white males."

So communist and capitalist, Russian and American, can establish solidarity via skin color if nothing else and become brothers in genocide. As befits such a global conspiracy in a high-tech era, this war against people of color must be fought covertly, with the desired results camouflaged to resemble natural disasters or the unforeseen consequences of social factors like poverty, unemployment, crime, imprisonment, drugs, and AIDS.

While Welsing sees every misfortune that strikes black people, whether in Africa or America, as deliberate, she soft-pedals historic acts of black aggression against whites. In discussing the Moorish invasion of Spain, for example, she refers to the dark-skinned African Moors as having "damaged" the pure white genes of the native whites. In this euphemism for rape, Welsing tries to make it sound as if the Moors had been merely inconsiderate. She maintains that there is no historical record of blacks ever aggressing against whites, yet neglects the frequent attempts by Islamic forces (since Welsing considers Arabs as well as Moors to be "colored" people) to invade, conquer, and impose their religion, culture—and genes—on Christendom.

Throughout her book, Welsing makes much of the alleged compensatory behavior of whites to banish their fear of genetic inadequacy and inferiority, yet her own audacious theory amounts to the same for blacks. She is particularly extravagant when she lauds black women as "the mothers of all mankind . . . the alpha and the omega of women on this planet. They were here in the beginning . . . they will be here in the end." She exhorts her sisters to be "African warrior-queens" and not "Cooperating Cleopatras." Queen Cleopatra, Welsing contends, was a black woman who unwittingly destroyed Egypt's pure African culture by politically and sexually associating with white Romans. This canard on Cleopatra's race is typical of Afrocentric historical revisionist logic: Cleopatra was queen of Egypt; Egypt is in Africa; therefore, Egypt was a black civilization, and Cleopatra therefore had to be black.

Such "noble lying" has been a staple of Afrocentric ideology ever since Marcus Garvey (who wanted to resettle American blacks in Africa) sanctioned it decades ago. And far from the Freudian-Einsteinian genius that she flatters herself to be, Welsing is more the black militant self-help guru, a faith-healer selling quack Afrocentric nostrums to a fractured community desperate for the solace of a glorious antique heritage and an even more glorious future renaissance. And if the result of this should be a malevolent black master-racism, it should come as no surprise considering that Welsing seriously believes that blacks "are inherently more than equal" to whites because of their very skin color or, more exactly, the high amounts of melanin in their skin pigmentation.

Melanin enrichment is to Welsing "the neurochemical basis for soul," just as white melanin deficiency is "the neurochemical basis for evil." In this Naziesque theorizing, Welsing posits melanin as being "a possible neurotransmitter and the skin melanocytes as the foundation of the sixth sense—the basis for knowledge of the unseen, including a deeper knowledge of 'bad.'" In her "Cress Theory on the George Washington Carver Phenomenon," Welsing seriously

suggests that the reason why the famed black scientist was so successful in his work with plants was because the skin melanocytes in
the "high level concentration of melanin skin pigment" of his dark
skin "enabled him to communicate with the energy frequencies
emanating from plants. Thus, he was able to learn their secrets and
purposes."

Welsing is not alone in taking such racist mysticism seriously. She
presented this theory at the first Melanin Conference held in 1987.
Welsing is included among the so-called "Melanin Scholars." Some
members of this group helped produce the controversial African
American Baseline Essays, which are now required teaching materials in some of the school districts (like Portland, Oregon's) that have
placed heavy emphasis on multicultural studies. This idea has
seeped into the mainstream of black culture, where casual
references to "superior melanin" are as common as Nation of
Islam–derived references to "knowledge of self."

Welsing's ideas have moved from the fringes of the Afrocentric
underground to the politically correct halls of the academy and now
into the wider mainstream, even into the corporate world. In a
recent issue of GQ, an account of the mandatory "sensitivity workshop" white males at one workplace were forced to undergo
portrayed one black female "facilitator" confronting her captives
with Welsing's cross symbolism theory, screaming at them its hidden
meaning of white "fear of black men on white women."

Crackpot Afrocentrism in the boardroom. Now there's something
to set your teeth on edge.

THE NEW RACISM

Racism in Academia

I am writing this essay sitting beside an anonymous white male that I long to murder." When I read this sentence, I found myself looking around the room nervously. Was there someone hiding with a weapon? Was this sentiment aimed at me?

Such paranoia might be occasioned by the opening of a new novel by Brett Easton Ellis. But what I am reading is actually an essay by bell hooks (the lowercase affectation is hers), a writer of wide-ranging influence in the university culture. Previously on the faculty of Yale, hooks is currently the Distinguished Professor of English at City College in New York, where there must be many nervous white males. Her recent collection of academic essays, *Killing Rage,* is one of eight similar diatribes that make up the *oeuvre* of a writer whom the *New York Review of Books* recently described as "the most prominent exponent of black feminism" in America.

The actual provocation for hooks' homicidal urge turns out to be nothing more than a lost seat in first class on a commercial airline's flight. Hooks tells how she had seated herself alongside a female friend, who is also black but identified only as "K." No sooner are hooks and her friend settled, however, than a voice over the plane's speaker system calls K to the front of the cabin, where her ticket is inspected and it is determined that she does not actually have a legitimate claim to the seat. This mishap is apparently the result of a faulty

upgrade, which it is too late to correct. At this time, K is also introduced to the anonymous white male of hooks' murderous intention,
who is holding the appropriately designated ticket and takes possession of K's seat, saying he is sorry to see her inconvenienced. Resign-
ing herself to the inevitable, K goes to relocate herself in coach.

Hooks is outraged. Unwilling to give up her own first-class
accommodation to join her friend, the professor turns her attention
to the white stranger: "I stare him down with rage, tell him that I do
not want to hear his liberal apologies, his repeated insistence that 'it
was not his fault.' I am shouting at him that it is not a question of
blame, that the mistake was understandable, but that the way K was
treated was completely unacceptable, that it reflected both racism
and sexism." Whitey, no liberal wimp, attempts to defend himself.
He lets her know "in no uncertain terms" that he feels the apology
he has already made is enough and that the professor "should leave
him be to sit back and enjoy his flight."

But this black Madame Defarge will have none of it: "In no
uncertain terms I let him know that he had an opportunity to not be
complicit with the racism and sexism that is so all-pervasive in
this society (that he knew no white man would have been called on
the loud-speaker to come to the front of the plane while another
white male took his seat)." *Say what?* "Yelling at him I said, 'It was
not a question of your giving up the seat, it was an occasion for you
to intervene in the harassment of a black woman.'"

Her invective exhausted, hooks takes out a pad and starts to pen
the notes from which she later composes this account. "I felt a 'killing
rage,'" she remembers. "I wanted to stab him softly, to shoot him
with the gun I wished I had in my purse. And as I watched his pain, I
would say to him tenderly 'racism hurts.'" While hooks is thinking
these tender thoughts, her intended victim senses the smoldering
hostility aimed in his direction. "The white man seated next to me
watched suspiciously whenever I reached for my purse. As though I
were the black nightmare that haunted his dreams, he seemed to be
waiting for me to strike, to be the fulfillment of his racist imagination.

I leaned towards him with my legal pad and made sure he saw the title written in bold print: 'Killing Rage.'"

Two pages after recounting this bizarre episode, now a text about racial oppression in the academy of radical thought, hooks makes the following observation: "Lecturing on race and racism all around this country, I am always amazed when I hear white folks speak about their fear of black people." Like other radicals, hooks is unable to connect the aggression she projects to the reaction she provokes. Her unwitting self-revelation is actually a paradigm of the radical mind in relation to the America it loves to hate.

Since we all have a bleeding heart, however well disguised, I searched in vain through hooks' text to find a reasonable source for her killing rage, one that would reach beyond the trivia of this occasion, one that would render her outburst less embarrassing not only for her, but also for her publisher, her university, and her admiring legions. But my search was truly in vain. I found no litany of racial incidents—not even the invocation of a past involving relatives who were slaves or victimized by the Klan or enmeshed in the criminal justice system—that might justify murderous thoughts or even the verbal abuse of a stranger, whose guilt seems, in hooks' own rendering, not only abstract but also debatable. Nothing. Nothing but homogenized anger and a passion torn to tatters.

Still a relatively young woman, hooks has already achieved the kind of academic fame and institutional validation that any of her peers, white or black, would envy, including a six-figure income and global itinerary (flying first class). Her lectures on "white supremacy" and related "black feminist" battle themes take her all over America and Europe, where she is able to advance her cause not in the usual coffeehouse bunkers of political vanguards, but in the cathedrals of the high culture, her expenses gratefully paid by administrators of venerable colleges, convinced, apparently, that their flocks could use a stiff dose of killing rage.

All this success, all the honors and intellectual power conferred, do not cause the slightest hesitation for hooks, who, like so many other fawned-over and spoiled black intellectuals, just won't take yes for an answer. As she explains, "My rage intensifies because I am not a victim." Like other radicals, hooks is eager to have her cake and eat it too, to accumulate the privileges of the comfortable while enjoying the moral gratification that comes with posturing as a champion of the afflicted, to wear the disinterested mantle of the scholar and still be a warrior for partisan causes.

Of course, it occurred to me almost instantaneously after reading that weird first sentence of her book that if hooks were not radical and black, her confession about wanting to kill would have provoked alarm. (Just as, if O. J. Simpson were white and his victims black, it is inconceivable that he would be playing golf today.) Interracial homicide, when contemplated by whites, is still a serious matter. But in the prevailing liberal ethos, black killing rage against whites must never be understood as individual pathology, but always as the redress of historical grievances or, as many blacks actually do seem to regard it, morally justified "payback." In the progressive view, as espoused by tenured radicals like bell hooks, it is even a necessary stage on the path to "liberation." The development of a proper killing rage is, in fact, not only politically correct but also morally salutary for the oppressed if they are not supinely to submit to their fate.

The repression of killing rage, as professor hooks informs us, is the agenda not of psychiatrists and peacemakers, as one might expect, but of white supremacists: "To perpetuate and maintain white supremacy, white folks have colonized black Americans, and a part of that colonizing process has been teaching us to repress our rage, to never make them the targets of any anger we feel about racism." White students who may resist such claims by their professor are advised to consult special texts: "When such conflicts arise," she informs her academic peers, "it is always useful to send students to read *Yours in Struggle*" (a 1944 book of three feminist perspectives on anti-Semitism and racism by Elly Bulkin, Minnie Bruce Pratt, and Barbara Smith). The term *struggle* actually understates the situation as hooks and her comrades construct it. What is really happening in America is an "on-going Black genocide and the patriarchy's war against women." Rage, in these circumstances, is not only "healing" but is also "revolutionary." Better still, it is self-defense. Blacks who lack rage are merely allowing themselves to be victims of the genocidal campaign that white America is waging against them: "When we embrace victimization, we surrender our rage."

This particular thought introduces a companion meditation, which constitutes the second essay in hooks' text and which is about a black man who did not surrender his rage. Colin Ferguson was a sometime college student (perhaps even a reader of professor hooks' texts), the scion of a prosperous Jamaican family. Ferguson made himself a footnote in the text of every radical Clausewitz on the subject of race war with his armed rampage on a Long Island commuter train, intended, as he explained in a note, to avenge "racism by Caucasians and Uncle Toms." The deranged Ferguson managed to kill six people, all Asian or white. (But nobody, I think, ever referred to him as a black "genocidal racist"—a term apparently reserved for white police officers who use the "N-word" in talking the talk, although, unlike Ferguson, they don't walk the walk.) The Ferguson tragedy could easily qualify as a text for a sermon on the dangers in attempting to justify a race-directed rage. Yet no one, least of all bell hooks, has mounted the pulpit. Consequently, the enraged and deranged Ferguson is, in certain quarters, catching on as a revolutionary hero instead. Martin Simmons, an instructor in English at New York University, was quoted in a recent *Vanity Fair:* "I have colleagues who tell me they're putting his picture on the wall next to Malcolm X."

Instead of preaching against the Long Island commuter massacre, professor hooks uses it as another occasion for renewing *her* racial rage, which she cossets with a narcissistic fervor. As hooks interprets the semiotics of the incident, it becomes a text on how the *white media* have turned Ferguson's deed into a racially charged image: "Even though the gunman carried in his pocket a list containing the names of male black leaders, the white-dominated mass media turned his pathological expression of anger towards blacks and whites into a rage against white people." She can't deny that he did set out to attack the white oppressor, but Ferguson also had a "complex understanding of the nature of neo-colonial racism," which the press deliberately obscured: "He held accountable all the groups who help perpetuate and maintain institutionalized racism, including black folks [that is, Uncle Toms]." By manipulating the facts, the white media were able to turn the tragedy into "a way to stereotype black males as irrational, angry predators," instead of an occasion "to highlight white supremacy and its potential 'maddening impact.'"

This task was left to attorney William Kunstler, the late radical advocate of the criminal and oppressed, who offered to defend Ferguson using the "black rage theory." Kunstler argued that white society drives black people into a homicidal rage for which they are not responsible. Ferguson, according to Kunstler, was "not responsible for his own conduct . . . white racism is to blame." A *National Law Journal* survey taken at the time found that two-thirds of blacks interviewed agreed with Kunstler's "black rage" theory.

Professor hooks offers her own supportive anecdotal insight: "In the aftermath of the train incident, I heard many well-off black people express their identification with the killer." She herself did not take any pleasure in the racial murders, but she does appear to enjoy reporting that she "heard many wealthy and privileged black folks express pleasure. These revelations surprised me since so many of these folks spend their working and intimate lives in the company of white colleagues."

Most blacks who harbored such feelings kept them to themselves, at the time. But some did not. During a rally held at Howard University, the Harvard of black colleges, Nation of Islam spokesman Khalid Muhammad compared the psychopathic Ferguson to rebel slave leader Nat Turner. Muhammad told a cheering, laughing audience of middle-class black students: "God spoke to Colin Ferguson and said, 'Catch the train, Colin, catch the train.'"

Like other Americans who do not happen to be black, I didn't get much of a yuck out of this obscenity. Yet if I can't say that it struck me as funny, I will allow that Muhammad's statement had significance. Reactions like this and the elation that followed the acquittal of the obviously guilty O. J. Simpson in the black community make hooks a telling witness about what has recently seemed like an epidemic of black racial hatred. Studies conducted at the Million Man March called by Nation of Islam leader Louis Farrakhan in November 1995 reveal that 40 percent of the participants had college educations and incomes exceeding $50,000, and that over 70 percent had incomes of more than $25,000 and were thus also solidly middle class. Farrakhan is now the most popular black leader among educated blacks, and he and his subordinate Khalid Muhammad are easily the most coveted and well-paid speakers before black student associations across the country. Inviting black racists to college campuses in defiance of white sensitivities has become, in fact, a rite of African American authenticity for black student groups everywhere.

Nor can it be dismissed as mere accident that—in contrast to the historical experience of all other ethnic groups—it is educated and middle-class members of the black community who are the most hospitable to the genocidal racism and anti-Semitic rantings of Farrakhan, Muhammad, and the followers of their cult. What other ethnic community in America would march one million strong behind their anti-Semites and racists? The Ku Klux Klan can't even assemble a public demonstration of its members that exceeds 100 or escape counter-demonstrations that outnumber its own 50 to 1.

Equally striking in this situation is the general tolerance for racist outrage when committed by blacks. Not long after the Million Man March, a white man was burned alive by blacks in Chicago, a pregnant white welfare mother and her two white children were murdered by three blacks who ripped a black fetus out of her womb in Illinois, seven whites were torched by a black racist in Harlem after protests against the very presence of the white-owned store they were in, and a black city worker in Fort Lauderdale gunned down five white coworkers, without a single acknowledgment by any public figure or the nation's press that the black community might have its own racial problem.

Actually this anomaly—the epidemic of middle-class black rage and the absence of corresponding outrage on the part of public officials and the liberal press when confronted by black racism—is grounded in a perception of America's race problem that was first announced some thirty years ago in the wake of the riots that afflicted Watts, Detroit, and other inner cities in the mid-sixties. It is a perception that became passé in the seventies but has now returned with a vengeance. This is the idea that it is not so much actual racists, let alone legal discrimination, that create a serious problem for black America as it is "institutional racism," a subtle but pervasive influence on social opportunity and behavior.

Institutional racism is an idea that originated as a phrase in a government report on the Watts riot, became part of the New Left worldview, and has recently reemerged in the "multicultural" academy, where it has metastasized in an elaborate body of pseudo-social-scientific cant in which any statistical disparity of black representation anywhere in the culture can be presented as proof of white malevolence and the necessity for preferential remedies. (One such academic "study" appeared in the *International Journal of Social Psychiatry*, where it was alleged that "institutional racism" was the major factor in the high incidence of schizophrenia found in Jamaicans who lived in the United States and England.)

In a time like our own when serendipities like Mark Fuhrman are rare, the idea of "institutional racism" is obviously a godsend for black demagogues fearful of going out of business. This theory keeps the dream alive. While slightly more respectable than Farrakhan's crackpot religious explanations (whites are "devils" invented by a mad scientist named Yacub), the theory of institutional racism inspires no less sweeping indictments of white depravity.

The unspoken assumption of every affirmative action policy is that institutions where whites predominate must be coerced into being fair to black applicants. But does even the most fanatical advocate of quotas believe that Harvard, Yale, and other institutions of the liberal elite would be contriving to keep qualified African American students from entry in the absence of affirmative action laws? Then why are such laws necessary? Because, their proponents argue, the influence of "institutional racism" is so subtle and so deeply ingrained that admissions officers at Harvard and Yale would exclude African Americans without realizing what they were doing.

The all-purpose concept of "institutional racism" originated with the Kerner Commission Report following the urban riots of the sixties. It was an attempt to explain—and to justify—the paradox of a rebellion against a legal system that had just achieved equality before the law (in the Civil Rights Acts of 1964 and 1965) for all Americans. This was the moment that ushered in what might be called the second civil rights era, whose most distinguishing achievement has been the squandering of the moral legacy of the first and the restructuring of the civil rights agenda around victimization and ever escalating demands for "redress of past injustice" as a radical cause. The pivotal legislation of this cause has been the system of racial preferences that is subsumed under the rubric of "affirmative action."

It is because the theory of institutional racism and the affirmative action policies it has spawned are a radical rejection of the American system—of individual rights, equal opportunity, and a single legal standard—that the most dramatic anomaly of the second civil rights era has been produced: Whereas the civil rights movement under Martin Luther King achieved its aims with the support of most American citizens and 90 percent majorities in both houses of

Congress, the current civil rights agenda—in so far as it is based on concepts such as collective guilt and institutional racism—is *opposed* by a majority of the American public and lawmakers. This opposition reflects the inability of most Americans to accept the double standard and to understand the persistence of "black rage" in the face of enormous social, cultural, and economic gains by African Americans and their own sense that they accept African Americans as full partners in America's civic compact. This sense of themselves, moreover, is corroborated by every major opinion survey on race relations—all showing unprecedented levels of acceptance by white America of its black citizens.

Why, as actual racial prejudice declines among white Americans, has black anger increased? The ubiquitous answer given by the civil rights Left is *institutional racism*. The failure of the rest of America to genuflect in response has spawned the peculiar angst of bell hooks and her comrades. "Why," writes hooks, "is it so difficult for many white folks to understand that racism is oppressive not because white folks have prejudicial feelings about blacks (they could have such feelings and leave us alone) but because it is a *system* that promotes domination and subjugation?" (emphasis added). Echoing hooks' complaint is another icon of the radical academy, longtime Communist Party leader Angela Davis. Interviewed in a 1996 double issue of the *New Yorker* devoted to race relations, Professor Davis laments the passing of the sixties, when "there was a great deal of discussion about . . . the importance of understanding the *structural* components of racism. There was an understanding that we couldn't assume that racism was just about prejudice—which, unfortunately, is what not only conservatives but liberals are arguing today" (emphasis added).

For radicals like hooks and Davis, whose greatest fear is obviously that they will be deprived of the rage that is the basis for their *schtick*, racism is no longer about prejudice (which, though still present, is clearly on the wane) but about *all* disparities between blacks and whites (each lumped together as one racial category despite the enormous disparity within those groups). Just as Marxists are convinced that class oppression exists when everyone is not economically equal, so race radicals know that racial oppression exists when any statistical disparity crops up between racial groups—as long, of course, as the disparity works against the "oppressed." No one, for example, argues that the over-representation of blacks in sports is the result of institutional racism and requires a government remedy. The fact that, according to the *Los Angeles Times*, a majority of the doughnut shops in California are owned by Cambodians also fails to elicit proposals for affirmative action for non-Cambodians who are excluded.

Unhappily, the racialist view of American social institutions is not just a matter of left-wing opinion but is incorporated into a body of law as well. Not since the segregationist era has the buttressing of a racialist philosophy been the work of American law schools. But now, at Harvard, Stanford, and other founts of academic legal scholarship, representatives of the school of "critical race theorists" argue that blacks can do no wrong and whites can do no right. Setting about the work of developing the theory of institutional racism, these law professors defend the importance of a "race-conscious perspective." They elaborate upon the theory that only whites can be racist (because "only whites have power") and even go so far as to defend common black criminals as rebels against an oppressive system (while of course deploring the effects of black-on-black crime). Not since Germany in the thirties have such clearly racialist doctrines been promulgated from the elite institutions of a nation and the inner sancta of its laws.

Not surprisingly, the theme of institutional racism was the text of Jesse Jackson's rant at the Million Man March: "We've come here today because there is a structural malfunction in America. It was structured in the Constitution and they referred to us as three-fifths of a human being, legally. There's a structural malfunction. That's why there's a crack in the Liberty Bell. There's a structural malfunction; they ignored the Kerner Report. Now we have the burden of two Americas: one half slave and one half free." (In which half does Jackson, a celebrity millionaire, locate himself?)

The utility of "structural" racism for demagogues like Jackson is that, while recognizing that the vast majority of whites are no longer overtly racist, they can use it to make all whites guilty nonetheless. No one has to be a racist in actual thought or deed to *participate* in a racist system or reap its benefits. Since the system "benefits" whites most (because statistically they have the greatest success), only whites, as a group, can properly be called its beneficiaries. Only whites can have power. And, therefore, only whites can be racist.

In understanding this tortured logic, bell hooks is an unfailing guide. Like Farrakhan and other radicals, she prefers the term *white supremacy* to *racism* in describing the enemy—because the latter suggests a search for individual culprits, when it is the system that is at fault. Professor hooks tells us that the revelation that led to her use of the term came when she encountered white women in the feminist movement who were not racist in the traditional sense. They actually sought the comradeship of blacks but still "wished to exercise control over our bodies and thoughts as their racist ancestors had." Whatever specifics lie behind this paranoid image of body-and-thought control (hooks doesn't provide details), the emotional bottom line is clear: As long as hooks feels less powerful in *any* relationship she has with whites—and for *whatever* reason—she will regard herself as a victim of racism. One suspects that many successful blacks see racists under the bed from similar impulses and for similar reasons respond favorably to racist incitements like Louis Farrakhan's claim to the million men he assembled in Washington that "the number one problem in the world is white supremacy."

Once accepted, of course, the concept of institutional racism is so powerful that blacks who embrace it are not only insulated from the charge of their own racism, but exculpated *in advance* for any crime they might commit. Thus hooks, in a kind of preemptive jury nullification, finds herself innocent of the murder she wanted to perpetrate: "Had I killed the white man whose behavior evoked that rage, I feel that it would . . . have been caused by . . . the madness engendered by a pathological context."

When blacks commit crimes, the truly guilty party is always the racist system that made them do it. Which is why even otherwise law-abiding blacks could celebrate the release of a double murderer like O. J. Simpson as "getting a brother off." Even when hooks does not identify with an odious African American deed, she finds a way to extenuate it. When dealing with Farrakhan's anti-Semitic poisons, for example, which she does not endorse and which even make her uncomfortable, she asks:

> From whom do young black folks get the notion that Jews control Hollywood? This stereotype trickles down from mainstream white culture. . . . Indeed, if we were to investigate why masses of black youth all over the United States know who Louis Farrakhan is, or Leonard Jeffries, we would probably find that white-dominated mass media have been the educational source. . . .
> So, . . . if the white media did their job and censored black leaders like Farrakhan he would have no black followers.

Of course, hooks' reasoning is so incoherent and circular that she could just as well blame the "white-dominated media" for *giving* blacks the impression that America is institutionally racist, since the media have bought the radical theory lock, stock, and barrel. To cite one illustrative case: A front page "news article" in the *Los Angeles Times*, January 10, 1993, purported to show that the traditional ladder of upward mobility for America's minorities no longer existed, thanks to institutional racism. The unspoken subtext of the article was that if this opportunity didn't exist, then—without affirmative action—none would:

Whether they have dropped out of high school or invested years in a graduate degree, whether they have struggled to master English or not, California's minorities earn substantially less than Anglos—a disparity that challenges the long-held tenet that education is a key to equality.

This "study," as reported by the *Times*, was probably more powerful in persuading middle-class blacks who read it that the system was stacked against them than all the speeches of Louis Farrakhan put together. But although the *Times* study was conducted from actual census figures by the newspaper's own statistical analyst, it showed nothing of the kind. The ethnic categories used in the analysis were "Anglo," "black," "Latino," and "Asian." But the category "Anglo" actually included a host of minorities—Jews, Armenians, and Arabs to name a few—who themselves are victims of ongoing hate crimes and discrimination, yet—for reasons unexplained in the study—provide its yardsticks of success. The oppressed categories were also suspiciously stacked. "Latinos," for example, is a spurious grouping that includes South American Indians and descendants of Spanish conquistadors, Portuguese-speaking Brazilians, low-income Puerto Ricans, and high-income Cubans.

In addition, the *Times* analysis made no allowance for the kind of educational degrees, graduate or otherwise, that the targets of its study possessed. Finally, the *Times* analysts made no allowance for age or on-the-job experience, critical components of earning potential. Yet the *Times* printed useless statistics and a racially inflammatory story nonetheless and probably felt that it was doing the right thing in confirming the existence of institutional racism. I actually was incensed enough when I read the story to call the reporters, who sheepishly admitted that they did not have sufficient data to make the claims they had but defended the decision to print them anyway, employing the Tawana Brawley theory of truth: Even if the article was wrong, it was right.

The concept of institutional racism, devised by radical academics and promoted by an irresponsible media, has led directly to another expression of oppressed rage called "black liberation theology." Its chief text, written by James Cone, is published by the Maryknoll Press. Cone came to the conclusion that even if whites were not individually racist, white racism was so oppressive to blacks that whites should be obliterated anyway:

> Most whites . . . do believe in "freedom in democracy," and they fight to make the ideals of the Constitution an empirical reality for all. It seems that they believe that, if we just work hard enough at it, this country can be what it ought to be. But it never dawns on these do-gooders that what is wrong with America is not its failure to make the Constitution a reality for all, but rather its belief that persons can affirm whiteness and humanity at the same time. This country was founded for whites and everything that has happened in it has emerged from the white perspective. . . . What we need is the destruction of whiteness, which is the source of human misery in the world.

This kind of Afro-Nazism would seem hard to swallow even for bell hooks. But she manages to gobble it down without difficulty: "Cone wanted to critically awaken and educate readers so that they would not only break through denial and acknowledge the evils of white supremacy, the grave injustices of racist domination, but be so moved that they would righteously and militantly engage in anti racist struggle." More likely they would simply take out their aggressions on the nearest white individual.

According to hooks, of course, this doesn't happen. "It is a mark of the way black Americans cope with white supremacy that there are few reported incidents of black rage against racism leading us to target white folks. . . . [Whites] claim to fear that black people will hurt them even though there is no evidence which suggests that black people routinely hurt white people in this or any other culture."

Actually there is. In 1994, according to U.S. Department of Justice statistics, there were 1.54 million violent crimes by blacks against whites. This contrasts with 187,000 violent crimes by whites against blacks, or one-fiftieth the rate, adjusted for relative population size.

Of course, the radical academics have institutional explanations for this depredation as well.

In a book that has already become a bible for the movement, Professor Andrew Hacker—a white professor with a politically correct "race conscious" perspective—discusses the fact that while blacks constitute only 12 percent of the population, they commit 43 percent of the rapes, including rapes of white women where (he is quick to emphasize) the risk to them is greater:

> Eldridge Cleaver once claimed that violating white women has political intentions. . . . Each such act brings further demoralization of the dominant race, exposing its inability to protect its own women from the worst kind of depredation. Certainly, the conditions black men face in the United States generate far more anger and rage than is ever experienced by white men. To be a man is made doubly difficult, since our age continues to associate "manliness" with worldly success. *If black men vent their frustrations on women, it is partly because the women are more available as targets, compared with the real centers of power, which remain so inchoate and remote.* (emphasis added)

For the sixties black radical as for the nineties white liberal, the act of rape—when committed by blacks—is no longer a vicious act against a defenseless individual—but an understandable attempt to strike out at the real culprit—the white supremacist *system*.

In the last analysis, all these arguments are really extensions of the Kerner Commission's attempt to use the concept of "institutional racism" to justify a civil riot. It should be no surprise that a most prominent member of the tenured black Left, Harvard professor Cornel West, a radical with even more stellar credentials than his one-time co-author, bell hooks, applauds the 1992 civil outrage in Los Angeles, which destroyed 58 lives and 2,000 Korean businesses (Koreans having been targeted by the black community as racial violators of its turf). West called this race riot a "monumental upheaval [that] was a multiracial, trans-class, and largely male display of justified social rage."

Racism, as bell hooks informs us, hurts. And the racists hurt not only the rest of us, but themselves as well. Indeed, the self-inflicted wound is often the real provocation for their rage. Returning to the incident on the plane flight that began her meditations, hooks reveals — without a hint of self-consciousness — just how the mishap depriving her friend of a first-class seat occurred. It began with a series of familiar urban frustrations (yes, bell, even whites have them). The professor, her antennae alert for manifestations of the white supremacist order, instantly converts each of these incidents into a call to arms:

> From the moment K and I had hailed a cab on the New York City street that afternoon we were confronting racism. The cabby wanted us to leave his taxi and take another; he did not want to drive to the airport. When I said that I would willingly leave but also report him, he agreed to take us.

They faced "similar hostility" when they stood in line for their first-class upgrades at the airport:

> Ready with our coupon upgrades, we were greeted by two young white airline employees who continued their personal conversation and acted as though it were a great interruption to serve us.

Impatient to be served, hooks interrupts the employees' conversation and is rebuffed by one of them, who interjects something like "Excuse me, but I wasn't talking to you." Hooks' response is to escalate her reaction until she creates an actual racial incident:

When I suggested to K that I never see white males receiving such treatment in the first-class line, the white female insisted that "race" had nothing to do with it, that she was just trying to serve us as quickly as possible.

Even the white female's effort to smooth over the situation is taken racially by hooks. She looks over her shoulder and sees that a line of "white men" has formed in back of them and concludes that to serve these privileged males her tormentors now "were indeed eager to complete our transaction even if it meant showing *no* courtesy." To spite them all, and make everyone wait anyway, hooks summons a supervisor to whom she again complains about the racism of the airline employees. The supervisor listens and apologizes, while the tickets are processed by the "white female." When the transaction is complete, hooks takes a cursory glance at the tickets she has obtained for herself and her friend K. She looks up quickly, however, to catch the hostility of the employee she has humiliated, commenting, "She looked at me with a gleam of hatred in her eye that startled, it was so intense."

Somewhere along the way through these emotional minefields, K's ticket has not been properly marked for upgrade, causing her to be "ejected" from her seat. She is replaced by the white male, who probably waited patiently in the same line behind them, without that healing rage, and got his ticket done correctly.

Professor hooks is a perfect expression of the misery the "multicultural" university has inflicted on itself and on the nation as a whole. The concept of institutional racism currently in vogue among hooks and her friends is an expression of racial paranoia, and nothing more. It is true that even paranoids have enemies. But it is also true that by projecting their insecurity and aggression onto those around them, paranoids create real enemies where there were none.

The Red and the Black

In the spring of 1985, in one of those self-betrayals Edgar Allan Poe defined as being controlled by "the imp of the perverse," Rutgers University president Francis Lawrence let slip his core belief that blacks must be given crumbs from the liberal table because they are genetically disadvantaged. This statement might have been dismissed as eccentric or even dangerously retrograde if it had not come from one of the leading social engineers in the contemporary university—someone who, while evidently believing that blacks were inferior, also tirelessly worked his administrative slide rule in behalf of diversity quotas. As it was, the uncomfortable conjunction of theory and practice elevated Lawrence's remark to the status of a metaphor that expressed with almost Euclidean perfection the moral bankruptcy of the multicultural university.

But at the same time that the episode at Rutgers was painting a depressing picture of the affirmative racism that infects higher education, an event was unfolding on the opposite coast, although with much less furor, that showed with equal precision how deeply mired in moral hypocrisy and intellectual sham the contemporary university has become. This event was the announcement by the chancellor of the University of California, Santa Cruz, that Angela Davis had been named to the Presidential Chair, the highest honor the university can bestow and one that carries an extra $30,000 a year for three years, along with coveted research assistance and other emoluments.

For many, Davis is merely a ghost of passions past. Indeed, in a 1990 interview with the *Los Angeles Times,* she said that the reason she pushed for ethnic studies classes was that she feared that her generation of radicals would be forgotten and that she dreaded the question she sometimes heard, "Angela Davis, is she still alive?" This was disingenuous of her, for she, like many of her old comrades, has found an afterlife in the university—first as a part-time teacher at San Francisco State University and then as a full professor at the University of California, Santa Cruz.

Davis is part of something called the Women of Color Research Cluster, which exists within something called the History of Consciousness Department. The names themselves sound like something from the course catalogue of the University of Mars, and they speak to the vulgarization that has overtaken American higher education in the last thirty years. But Davis's acceptance as a member in good standing of the academic community raises questions that transcend the trendy flakiness of the campus curriculum. Is allowing a laid-back Stalinist like Davis to teach "Critical Issues in 20th Century Marxism" any different from allowing a follower of the philosophy of Joseph Mengele to teach a course in surgical procedures?

Realizing they had cooked a hot potato in giving Davis a high honor, Santa Cruz administrators first said the funds from which she was being paid came from private sources and then had to backtrack and admit public moneys were part of the package. They then pointed out that the chair was awarded on the basis of proposals submitted by the candidates and it was therefore Davis's project (which, among other things, involves creating "alternatives to women's incarceration in California") rather than Davis herself who was being honored.

All this bureaucratic mumbling was actually the squid's ink that provides cover for an administrative getaway. It allowed Santa Cruz officials to dodge the big question: What is this woman doing in a tenured position on a University of California campus? Angela Davis, after all, has never made the slightest pretense of being engaged in the pursuit of the truth and doesn't even bother to identify herself as a teacher or scholar; rather, she calls herself a "political activist" whose life, in the Marxist narcissism that characterizes her self-inventory, has "been informed for almost two decades by local and global struggles for progressive social change."

Other radicals of the sixties had a perverse appreciation for the United States. Billy Ayres, onetime comrade of Bernadine Dohrn in the Weatherman terrorist sect and later her husband, expressed this view in his blithe look back at those heady days: "Guilty as hell, free as a bird, America's a great country." Angela Davis never had this childlike delight at discovering the forgetful and forgiving nature of her native land. For her, everything that happened was, naturally, historically inevitable. And to some degree she is right; there is a sort of Hegelianism in the way she—and we—got from the sixties to the nineties—as the radicals who had failed in their attempt to burn the university down decided to come back as graduate students on the "long march through the institutions" and eventually got on the tenure track and then on the hiring committees.

Davis had her fifteen minutes of fame in the sixties, but she was an anomalous figure even in that anomalous decade. While the other radicals of the day identified themselves as free spirits, anarchists, and poets of violence, for Davis, the first (indeed, the only) allegiance was to the Communist Party. What was for others a time of breaking loose was for her a time of boring from within. Her fate was set when in 1960, as a bright fifteen-year-old, she left her native Birmingham for New York on an AFS scholarship and found a mentor in Communist historian Herbert Aptheker (who had just recently provided an odious rationale for the invasion of Hungary) and a friend in Aptheker's daughter Bettina (who is now a colleague at Santa Cruz). At a time when other Communists, still reeling from the 1956 Khrushchev revelations about Stalin, were leaving the party in droves, Davis was signing on in a perverse gesture that mocked the sixties concept of "youthful idealism." For two years she hung out afternoons at the Aptheker house, but she and Bettina were not listening to Pat Boone records. They were creating a Communist youth organization called Advance. In her autobiography, Davis recalls at this time first reading *The Communist Manifesto*, which, she says, "hit me like a bolt of lightning." Judging by what came later, it did permanent damage.

Events of the next few years had the feel of a fast-track course for someone seeking to be ordained in the Communist priesthood. Going to the 1962 Communist Youth Festival in Helsinki, she agitated against the "warmonger" Kennedy and joined the Cuban conga line. Attending Brandeis on scholarship, she became a student of Herbert Marcuse's, and in 1965 she moved on to Frankfurt to do graduate work with Marcuse's colleague Theodor Adorno. In her autobiography she explains that while in Germany she decided to go to Berlin and naturally wanted to see Checkpoint Charlie. Standing there with her hidden agenda held tight within her, she listened scornfully to white tourists complaining about the long wait to go across and see the other side, then went to the front of the line, showed her passport, and was ushered right across. Of the benign guards of the German Democratic Republic, who were just then shooting anyone who tried to make the trip from East to West, she says: "This was their way of showing solidarity with black people."

After two years in Europe, she returned to Southern California to work on her Ph.D. and study again with Marcuse, who had moved (because of "political reasons," naturally) from Brandeis to the University of California at San Diego. She never got the degree, because she began to spend time in the black revolution as part of the efforts of the Communist Party of the United States to exert influence in that movement. She started with the Student Nonviolent Coordinating Committee but quit in disgust when that organization wisely began expelling the Communists, who, it felt, were trying to take over. She then went into the Che-Lumumba Club, the black Communist cell in Southern California, and became involved with the Black Panthers, conducting political education tutoring illiterate cadre in Lenin's *State and Revolution*.

Moving on from the Panthers, Davis got involved in the prisoner movement in late 1969, specifically in the movement to free George Jackson and the two other Soledad Brothers. She fell in love with Jackson, who was just then being lionized as the "revolutionary poet" by Jean Genet and others, although he was actually a psychopath who gave piquancy to his myth by admitting to his closest supporters that he'd killed a dozen men in prison. After what some members of the Soledad Brothers Defense Committee described as brazen sexual encounters in the visitors' area, Davis found herself the recipient of some of Jackson's most erotic letters.

Her Communism never would have made Davis a national figure, but her involvement with the "black liberation struggle" growing out of the prisoners' movement did. She jumped into the spotlight in the spring of 1970 when it was alleged that she was the source of the guns George Jackson's seventeen-year-old brother Jonathan used in his bloody assault on the Marin County Courthouse in 1970. During the action, an effort to free George, Jonathan Jackson blew Superior Judge Harold Haley's head off with a shotgun owned by Davis; and this touched off a nationwide hunt for her. Davis was finally apprehended in New York after several weeks on the lam. Entering what she calls "The Period of My Persecution," she denied supplying the guns and loudly insisted that she would never get a fair trial, which may have been right, since she was soon acquitted by an all-white jury in Marin County. Immediately after being released, she went on a victory lap back to East Germany and the Soviet Union and then accepted Fidel Castro's invitation to go to Cuba and write her autobiography.

This episode gave her ambiguous status as one of the icons of the sixties—a handsome woman whose backlit Afro circled her head like a halo. She was a major asset to the party in its efforts to infiltrate the black radical movement. After the sixties self-destructed, she kept a hand in this movement while also pressing for a popular front with other "progressives" to support Soviet moves into Africa and Central America and to defeat U.S. attempts to counter this new

174

THE NEW RACISM

imperialism. She was Gus Hall's vice-presidential candidate on the Communist ticket in 1980 and 1984, someone always ready to use the afterglow of her sixties celebrity to shill for Soviet interests— whether it was justifying the brutal war in Afghanistan or sneering at the claims of Soviet dissidents that Jews were mistreated in the USSR. (When Alan Dershowitz once asked her to speak up in behalf of these political prisoners, Davis had her *secretary* inform him that in her opinion they were all "Zionist fascists and opponents of socialism" and ought to be locked down even harder.)

What we have here, in short, is not someone mastering a scholarly subject or honing her teaching skills or creating the major work that was once thought to be the foundation of an academic career. This is rather the curriculum vitae of a party hack who got her passport stamped at every gray and depressing junction along the party line. And, in fact, Angela Davis never left the Communist Party; it left her when she and other black communists were purged by Gus Hall late in 1991, long after even most of the Soviet apparatchiks had left the party. The specifics of that fractious Communist Party meeting in Cleveland are hard to come by—even expelled members being unwilling to wash their dirty Lenin in public—but it appears that Davis was not, as she later claimed, in the forefront of the delayed partisans of *glasnost* trying to open the Communist Party of the United States to "democracy." Her quarrel with Hall seems to have come about because she tried to force on party leadership the racial quotas that she saw working so well within the university, and he refused to name the requisite numbers of blacks and women to leadership positions.

In 1992, her mentor, Herbert Aptheker, who was expelled along with her, finally condemned the Soviets after serving them for sixty years. Davis never did. She just began to graze in the greener pastures of the university, where no apologies for radical passions are expected, first at San Francisco State and then at Santa Cruz, where she joined her old comrade Bettina Aptheker after a stealth appointment in 1991 that still baffles some staff members there. (Aptheker is now teaching women's studies in courses claiming that lesbianism is the highest stage of feminism.) Davis has spritzed up her image with a hint of the New Age, stopping a four-pack-a-day cigarette habit and becoming a runner and vegetarian, trading the Afro for equally stunning dreadlocks, and moving into the gay movement as a "minister" who, according to the San Francisco *Bay Guardian*, has performed lesbian weddings in the Bay Area.

In defending the choice of Davis as Presidential Chair, Santa Cruz dean Gary Lease called her an "accomplished scholar and social critic trying to heal the wounds of an increasingly divided society." Only in the deconstructed university would such a fatuous remark fail to draw guffaws. The idea of trying to heal wounds was a particularly nice touch given the fact that, in sympathy demonstrations with the Los Angeles rioters in 1992, Davis told Santa Cruz students that private property should not necessarily be held as sacred when they left the campus to march on the city.

Outside of her autobiography, Davis has two books that Dean Lease might have had in mind in extolling her scholarship. The most recent, *Women, Race and Class* (1988), is actually not a book at all, but rather a compilation of speeches, often given at $10,000 a pop to standing ovations at places like Dartmouth, where Davis was hailed as a heroic figure by President James Friedman and his deans.

If her previous book, *Women, Culture and Politics* (1982), is scholarship, it is of a kind that was once produced in the USSR. It is not simply polemical but rather a tract filled with servile praise for the Soviet Union. In a chapter on the drudgery of housework faced by American women, for instance, Davis writes, "The only significant steps taken toward ending domestic slavery have in fact been taken in the existing socialist countries." (This when Soviet women were victimized by the most extreme sexism outside the Third World and treated like beasts of burden by their husbands and the state.) And in a chapter on the black family she says, "Observers of the current crisis within the black family might find it instructive to examine the present situation in some of the socialist countries

... [where] there is no semblance whatsoever of the soaring poverty associated with the increase of such families in the United States." (This at almost exactly the same time that Boris Yeltsin visited the U.S. and, during a tour of black neighborhoods in Washington, D.C., surprised his hosts by observing that what were called slums in America would qualify as comfortable housing in his homeland.)

While such work might fit quite nicely into the pages of *The People's World* or might justify the 1979 Lenin Peace Prize that, until the UC Presidential Chair, was Davis's highest honor, it is not scholarship in keeping with any institution of higher learning that pretends to take its mission seriously. No scholar, not even one who questioned U.S. involvement in Southeast Asia, would write, as Davis does, that it was the "policy" of the U.S. military command "to systematically encourage rape" by American soldiers in Vietnam "since it was an extremely effective weapon of mass terrorism." No scholar, not even one critical of U.S. social policy, would fill her work, as Davis does, with vulgar anti-Americanism and bathetic economic reductionism like the following: "It is no coincidence that a government that would sabotage the rights of every citizen in this country by permitting the development of a secret junta controlled by the CIA and the National Security Council also seriously infringed upon the health rights of black women and all poor people."

The sad truth of the matter is that only in the multicultural university—a place filled with chic nihilism about truth and merit, a place where double standards and mazes of special privilege are enshrined as policy, and a place where there is more talk about group membership and blood quantum than at any time since the Nuremberg Laws—could someone who writes and thinks like Angela Davis be given tenure, let alone a high honor. Only in the politically correct university could a refugee of a bankrupt faith like Davis find a field such as race-class-gender studies into which she could insinuate her discredited old agenda without missing a beat. Her adeptness in picking up the new lingo can be seen in her description of one of her courses: "A survey of the principle [sic] ideological issues of the

20th century; attitudes toward sex, race, class, work, violence and knowledge viewed from the perspective of structuralism and semiological theories of culture."

Davis's proponents suggest that any criticism of her is a veiled attack on academic freedom. But academic freedom was never intended to protect mediocrity, hidden agendas, or the venal adherence to party lines. Would those who think Angela Davis ought to be honored at Santa Cruz also agree that someone like David Duke should be given a tenured position and distinctions on their campus because he represents "a point of view"? Would these supporters argue that having a Stalinist teach social policy is any less obnoxious than allowing a Nazi to teach eugenics?

Historian Ronald Radosh, author of *The Rosenberg File* and a longtime student of the Communist Party, says, "Angela Davis is a fraud. Even the left-wing scholars don't bother to cite her. Nobody takes her seriously." Nobody, that is, except the administrators at UC Santa Cruz. On that campus she is now more equal than others.

The tragedy of Angela Davis's selection as Presidential Chair is that it did not involve administrators capitulating to pressure from below. There was no groundswell from students, no academic committee pumping enthusiastically for her selection. This was a decision made at the highest levels of the university, which suggests that administrators, who once merely mouthed others' radical pieties in an effort to keep the lid on, have been repeating the politically correct platitudes so long now that they have come to believe them.

And so it is that Rutgers president Francis Lawrence's slip of the tongue and UC Santa Cruz's appointment of Angela Davis to its highest honor come together in a sort of harmonic convergence that defines the tragedy of the contemporary university. The one episode is about the liberal racism that has remade the university in its image. The other is about the cynical replacement of standards of excellence by an intellectual fraud that is now so deeply embedded in the system it has become part of business as usual. Together they acquire a crushing weight.

Clarence Page's Race Problem, and Mine

C larence Page is a well-known television commentator, Pulitzer Prize–winning columnist for the *Chicago Tribune*, and author of the recent book *Showing My Color*. An adolescent in the civil rights era, Page's own significant achievement could be taken as a symbol of that era's success. Indeed, he has forcefully dissociated himself from the separatists of the Million Man March and—unlike his radical peers—is not ashamed of expressing hope in the American dream. Yet, in *Showing My Color*, Page has written an apologia for these same angry voices that calls into question the legacy of Martin Luther King and makes the author into a metaphor for the new black intellectual sensibility.

Page takes the title of his book from a frequently heard parental admonition of his youth: "Don't be showin' yo' color." Showing your color, he explains, "could mean acting out or showing anger in a loud and uncivilized way." More particularly it means to him playing to stereotype. In other words, "showing your color" really means showing your culture—an irony that escapes the author. The title, he explains, "emerged from my fuming discontent with the current fashions of *racial denial*, steadfast repudiations of the difference race continues to make in American life" (Page's emphasis). Page then attacks the " 'color-blind' approach to civil rights law" and laments the way the words of Martin Luther King have been "perverted" to support this view.

The argument of Page's book begins inauspiciously with a personal anecdote through which he intends to establish that racism is, indeed, a "rude factor" in his life and — by extension — the lives of all black Americans. For Page, it is the memory of a trip to Alabama in the fifties, where he encountered water fountains marked "colored" and "white." It does not occur to him that outrage over events from nearly fifty years ago has exhausted its shelf life. If you are forced to invoke a distant past to justify a present case, the case is already undermined.

Page remembers a moment of overt racism. But while acknowledging that such moments are probably behind us, he cannot let go altogether and, embracing the current fashion of black intellectuals, argues that a subtle and invisible set of power relationships continues to produce the same results: "Social, historical, traditional and institutional habits of mind that are deeply imbedded in the national psyche . . . work as active agents to impede equal opportunity for blacks." The (politically correct) name for these factors is "institutional racism":

> [Racism] is not just an internalized belief or attitude. It is also an externalized public practice, a power relationship that continually dominates, encourages, and reproduces the very conditions that make it so useful and profitable.

Though old-style racism has been conquered and is no longer an acceptable part of America's mainstream, an even more sinister "institutional racism" lives on as the defining fact of American life.

While retailing these clichés of the Left, Page insists on presenting his own psychodrama more complexly. True, he may be nominally a "progressive," but there is a conservative inside him struggling to get out: "Conservatism resonates familiarly with me, as I think it does with most black Americans." The fact that there is some truth in this self-description makes what Clarence Page has to say important (the chapter where it appears is pointedly called "A Farewell to Alms"):

> We vote liberal, for liberalism has helped us make our greatest gains. But in other areas, we swing conservative. We want to believe that hard work will be rewarded. . . . We want to believe in the promise of America.

It takes courage for Page to defend his conservative instincts, especially in view of the intimidating pressures within the black community to make visible representatives like him bow to racial solidarity on crucial issues. Thus Page does not hesitate to point out that the anti-Semitic ravings of Louis Farrakhan and other spokesmen for the Nation of Islam have created the public climate in which a Yankel Rosenbaum could be lynched in Crown Heights a few years ago and in which his killer could be acquitted by a jury of blacks.

Page remains a political Democrat, he claims, because of Republicans' assumption that "racism is no longer a problem" and their view "that government programs and agencies must be trimmed, even when those programs and agencies offer the last slender thread of protection the grandchildren of America's black slaves have against further slides back into oppression." In particular, he singles out conservative opposition to minimum-wage laws, affirmative action employment policies, and welfare aid to mothers with dependent children. But a deeper, cultural dimension to Page's differences with Republicans is evoked by sentences like this:

> Klan membership dropped sharply in the early 1980s, according to researchers for the Anti-Defamation League and other Klan-watching groups, as many found a new, satisfying voice and vehicle in Republican Party politics. Enter David Duke.

But Duke, whose influence (unlike Farrakhan's) does not reach outside Louisiana or into the chambers of Congress, was instantly proscribed by the Republican Party leadership, including three former Republican presidents, none of which does Page acknowledge. This lapse into partisan race-baiting provokes me into showing my own color. I am a Jewish Republican, who nearly fifty years ago marched in support of Harry Truman's Fair Employment Practices Act, and I have been active in civil rights struggles ever since. Moreover, I have a personal anecdote of anti-Semitism that is more current than Page's encounter with "white" and "colored" water fountains in the fifties. I am recently engaged to a non-Jewish woman, who has been confronted by several friends who have said, "How can you marry a Jew?"

The level of Jew hatred in America is higher today than it has been in my entire lifetime, thanks not only to the poisonous rant of Farrakhan but also to the collusion of large sections of the black intelligentsia in legitimizing his viewpoint for black Americans. It is black anti-Semites like Farrakhan, in fact, who have legitimated public anti-Semitism in a way that no other group in America could. Nor does it seem that Jews can afford to feel as protected today by the American mainstream as blacks can. When Marlon Brando launched an attack on Hollywood Jews on a Larry King show and went on to talk about "kikes," "chinks," and "niggers," it was only the "N-word" that got bleeped by the CNN censors. "Institutional racism," it seems, can cut more than one way.

Anti-Semitism has real-world consequences for Jews, just as surely as racism does for blacks. A Jew knows not to attempt a career in the auto business in Detroit, to cite one of many possible examples, without taking into account the fact that Jews have not done well in the auto industry and thus the hazards of such an effort. I have stood in the living rooms of Grosse Pointe mansions and felt the disdain caused by my ethnicity. But this does not lead me or my fellow Jews to call for government-enforced preferences for Jews or to seek the source of this prejudice in the institutional heart of the nation.

For a voting liberal, Page's familiarity with conservative writers is unusually broad, and his readings are mostly respectful. It is not surprising, therefore, that his defense of affirmative action is often shrewd. But for a conservative who does not fit the liberal caricature (angry white males threatened by minority advances), his arguments remain singularly unconvincing. Like other defenders of an indefensible policy, Page begins by denying that affirmative action is what it is:

> Despite myths to the contrary, affirmative action is not intended to pro-
> mote people who are not qualified. It is intended to widen the criteria
> for those who are chosen out of the pool of the qualified.

Unfortunately, for this argument, there are numerous and obvious examples that prove just the opposite. Journalist Roger Wilkins was made University Professor of History at George Mason University despite the fact that he had no qualifications as a historian, never having written a scholarly monograph in his life.

Wilkins was chosen, it happens, over my friend Ronald Radosh, who at the time had been a history professor for twenty years, had published widely in scholarly journals, and had also written several highly respected books in his field. Nor is Wilkins an isolated case. Julian Bond's failed political career has led for no apparent reason (other than the politics of race) to concurrent professorships at two universities (Virginia and Maryland), also in history. Cornel West and Angela Davis hold two of the highest paid and most prestigious university chairs in America, despite their intellectual mediocrity (in Davis's case, compounded by her disreputable career as a Communist Party apparatchik and lifelong apologist for Marxist police states). Indeed, the weakness of the affirmative action case is exposed by the very fact that its most intensely contested battlefields are elite universities, which rank among the nation's most liberal institutions. Page actually defends the beleaguered affirmative action programs at the University of California with the argument that enrollment levels of blacks are expected to drop when affirmative action is ended. Would Page have us believe that the admissions departments of liberal universities like the University of California are infested with angry white males conspiring to keep black enrollment down? Or with built-in "institutional biases" excluding blacks? The reality is that since 1957 when the California regents adopted their famous "Master Plan," every single California resident, regardless of race, who graduates from high school with certain achievements has been guaranteed a place in the university system. Matriculation from various points in the system, starting with community and junior colleges to positions at Berkeley and UCLA (its academic pinnacles), were based—until the advent of racial preferences—on grade point averages and achievement tests, and these alone.

By way of defending policies that trump grades with racial preferences, Page invokes the "geographical diversity" criteria of the Ivy League schools, commenting, "Americans have always had a wide array of exotic standards for determining 'merit.'" Page doesn't seem to realize that "geographical diversity" criteria were introduced to restrict the enrollment of Jews. Page even quotes, without irony, a "friend" who said he was convinced he got into Dartmouth because he was the only applicant from Albuquerque: "I'm sure some talented Jewish kid from New York was kept out so I could get in."

When I went to Columbia in the fifties, the Jewish enrollment with the geographical diversity program in place was 48 percent. That was the Jewish quota. We Jews were well aware of the anti-Semitic subtext of the geographical diversity program and talked about it openly. But we did not launch protests or seek government interventions to abolish the program. The opportunity that was offered seemed sufficient. Once the principle of Jewish admission was accepted, even residual (or "institutional") anti-Semitism could not keep Jews, who constituted only 3 percent of the population, from flooding the enrollment lists of Ivy League schools. Liberals like Clarence Page support affirmative action because they are in a state of massive denial. The problem of black enrollment at elite universities is not caused by racist admissions policies. It is caused by poor academic performance.

In defending affirmative action policies, Page reveals the under-lying element in most expressions of "black rage" these days. This is the displacement of personal frustrations, the unwillingness of many blacks to go through the arduous process that other ethnic minori-ties have followed in their climb up the American ladder. Thus Page opens his chapter on affirmative action with a personal anecdote. As a high school graduate in 1965, he applied for a summer newsroom job but was beaten out by a girl who was less qualified and younger, but white. Shortly after that, the Watts riot occurred and he was hired. Page's comment: "You might say that my first job in newspapers came as a result of an affirmative action program called 'urban riots.'"

This is a familiar cliché of the Left. White people respond fairly to blacks only when they have a gun to their heads. Thus Malcolm X, who scorned the civil rights movement (in a 1963 speech he re-ferred to "the recent ridiculous march on Washington" because he believed, wrongly, that Americans would never give blacks their rights), is seen in retrospect by many black intellectuals as the au-thor of the civil rights movement because his violent racism scared whites into agreement. But what is immediately striking in Page's re-flection is that he doesn't pause to consider that this was his first job application and that it was only for a summer position. Perhaps the men doing the hiring wanted to have a girl around the office for a couple of months. This would be an unprofessional rationale for the hiring, but not racist. Nor would it require a riot to remedy.

Page gives no thought to the possibility that he would have been hired eventually anyway. Recognizing that significant changes take time is not the same as saying that they require force to implement. Was it the threat of riots or of affirmative action laws that eventually made black athletes dominant in leagues whose owners (Marge Schott immediately comes to mind) hardly rank among the socially enlightened? Or that allowed black cultural artists to achieve an equally dominant position in the popular music industry? How did

Oprah Winfrey, a black sharecropper's daughter from Mississippi, become mother-confessor to millions of lower-middle-class white women (and a multi-millionaire in the process) without affirmative action? Page has no answer. And he doesn't even address the most profound implication of his anecdotal encounter with racism: The unfairness that touched him back in the mid-sixties has, in affirmative action, been systematized and elevated to a matter of national policy!

The primary reason most conservatives oppose affirmative action is one that is given almost no attention by progressives eager to attribute base motives to their opponents. Racial preference is an offense in principle to the core values of American pluralism, which depends on the neutrality of American government toward all its diverse communities. Affirmative action is a threat to inclusiveness, because privilege is established under affirmative action policy not by achievement, but by legal coercion. The principle of affirmative action, which is inevitably—and despite all demurrers—a principle of racial preference, is a threat to what Felix Frankfurter identified as "the ultimate foundation of a free society . . . the binding tie of cohesive sentiment." Affirmative action based on principles like geographical diversity constitutes no such threat, but policies based on race do. Affirmative action is a corrosive acid, eating at the moral and social fabric of American life. Every time a black leader refers to the paucity of blacks on the faculty of Harvard or in the upper reaches of corporate America, the automatic presumption is that white racism is responsible. The legal concept of "racial disparity" embodies the same assumption. The idea that government must compel its white citizens to be fair to its minority citizens presumes that white America is so racist it cannot be fair on its own account. This involves supporters of affirmative action in an illogic so insurmountable it is never mentioned: If the white majority needs to be forced by government to be fair, how is it possible that the same white majority—led by a Republican president named Richard Nixon—created affirmative action policies in the first place?

There is no answer to the question because, in fact, affirmative action was not created because of white racism. It was created because of widespread black failure to take advantage of the opportunities available when legal segregation was ended. Since the politics of the Left are premised on the idea that social institutions determine what happens to people, this failure had to be the result of institutional rather than individual factors.

If affirmative action "works," as Page implies, it does so in ways he does not mention. Looked at objectively, its primary achievement appears to have been to convince black Americans that whites are indeed so racist that some external force must compel their respect and, secondarily, that blacks need affirmative action in order to gain equal access to the American dream. The further consequence of this misguided "remedy" has been to sow a racial paranoia in the black community so pervasive and profound that even blacks who have benefited from America's racial generosity have been significantly affected in the way they think. How significantly is revealed in the almost casual way the paranoia surfaces:

"Black is beautiful" was the slogan which made many white people nervous, as any show of positive black racial identification tends to do.

Does it? The television mini-series *Roots*, after all, was one of the most significant milestones of positive black racial identification — an epic of black nobility and white evil purporting to represent the entire history of American race relations. It was not only produced and made possible by whites, but also voluntarily watched by more whites than any previous television show in history. Conversely, most of the negative stereotypes of blacks in today's popular culture are the work of black stars and directors like Martin Lawrence and Spike Lee. As far as the infamous "gangsta rap" industry, which celebrates black sociopathic behavior, goes, blacks own the most profitable labels.

In gauging the size of the chip ominously perched on black America's shoulders, few measures are so choice as the following passage:

> Black people may read dictionaries, but many see them as instruments of white supremacy. They have a point. Dictionaries define what is acceptable and unacceptable in the language we use as defined by the ruling class [*sic*]. . . . The dictionary's pleasant synonyms for "white" ("free from moral impurity . . . innocent . . . favorable, fortunate . . .") and unpleasant synonyms for "black" (". . . thoroughly sinister or evil . . . wicked . . . condemnation or discredit . . . the devil . . . sad, gloomy or calamitous . . . sullen . . . ") are alone enough to remind black people of their subordinate position to white people in Anglo-European traditions and fact.

This cliché has become bedraggled with overuse. Its major defect is not that it is outworn, but that it is self-defeating as far as Page's argument is concerned. White lexicographers had nothing to do with identifying Clarence Page and his racial kindred as "black" in the first place. When Page and I were young, blacks were called "Negroes" and had been called so for hundreds of years. The word *Negro* has no such negative connotations, moral or otherwise. It was Malcolm X who first embraced *black* as a term of pride, employing the word *Negro* to connote the white man's pliant black, the "Uncle Tom." After Malcolm's death, Stokeley Carmichael and the new radical civil rights leadership aggressively took up the label with the slogan "Black Power" and demanded that *black* be used as a sign of respect. The liberal cultural establishment obliged. It was only then acquiesced in by the majority of whites who, in fact, for more than a generation now have ardently wished that black America would finally get what it wanted from them (and be happy about it).

When all the layers are peeled from the discussion of "racism" in *Showing My Color*, we are left with a disappointing residue of hand-me-down Marxism:

188 THE NEW RACISM

Modern capitalist society puts racism to work, wittingly or unwittingly. It populates a surplus labor pool of last-hired, first-fired
workers whose easy employability when economic times are good
and easy disposability when times go bad helps keep all workers'
wages low and owners' profits high. . . . Racism is one of many non-
class issues, such as busing, affirmative action, or flag burning, that
diverts attention from pocketbook issues that might unite voters
across racial lines.

This is simple-minded, sorry stuff, unworthy of Clarence Page or
any other intellectual (black or otherwise). The problem with the
black underclass is not that it is underemployed, but unemployable.
Blacks who have fallen through society's cracks don't even get to the
point of being "last-hired." The flood of illegal Hispanic immigrants
into areas like South Central Los Angeles, displacing indigenous
blacks, shows that the jobs exist but that the resident black population either won't or can't take them. The fact that one in three
young black males in America is enmeshed in the criminal justice
system—a fact that Page doesn't begin to confront—doesn't help
their employability. Once again, the category of racism provides a
convenient shield for a massive denial of problems that have very
little to do, specifically, with race.

In fact, the racial conflict in America is being driven not by
economics or even white prejudice, but by radical political agendas—by Clarence Page's friends on the Left like Manning Marable,
Ronald Takaki, and Michael Lerner (all of whom have provided
blurbs for Page's book) and by their liberal allies who keep up the
drumbeat of complaint about American racism and "oppression."
The very phrase *institutional racism* is, of course, of leftist prove-
nance. It is also a totalitarian term. Like *ruling class*, it refers to an
abstraction, not a responsible individual being. You are a class
enemy (or, in this case, a race enemy) not because of anything you
actually think or do, but "objectively"—because you are situated in
a structure of power that gives you (white skin) privilege. Page is as-

tute enough to see that if racism is defined as an institutional flaw, "it does not matter what you think as an individual" and therefore such a definition offers "instant innocence" to the oppressor. But he is not shrewd enough to see that it imputes instant culpability as well. While absolving individual whites of guilt, it makes all whites guilty.

The belief in the power of institutional racism allows black civil rights leaders to denounce America as a "racist" society, when it is actually the only society on earth—black, white, brown, or yellow—whose defining creed is antiracist, a society to which black refugees from black-ruled nations regularly flee in search of opportunity and refuge. But the real bottom line is that the phantom of institutional racism allows black leaders to avoid the encounter with real problems within their own communities, which are neither caused by whites nor solvable by the actions of whites, but which cry out for attention.

The problem with the discontent now smoldering inside America's privileged black intellectuals, so well expressed in *Showing My Color*, is that it can never be satisfied:

> Nothing annoys black people more than the hearty perennial of black life in America, the persistent reality of having one's fate in America decided inevitably by white people. It is an annoyance that underlies all racial grievances in America, beginning with slavery, evolving through the eras of mass lynchings and segregated water fountains, and continuing through the age of "white flight," mortgage discrimination, police brutality, and the "race card" in politics.

In Page's view, the unifying and ultimate goal of all black reformers, whether radicals like bell hooks or conservatives like Clarence Thomas, is "black self-determination." What Clarence Page and blacks like him want is "to free the destiny of blacks from the power of whites."

Within a single national framework, this is obviously an impossible goal, and those who advocate it must know this. (Does Page want to go back to Stokeley Carmichael's ridiculous demand in the sixties for blacks to be given Mississippi?) The goal is precious to them precisely because it can never be realized and thus, to turn one of Jesse Jackson's cries on its head, it keeps rage alive. Those who push for "black self-determination" in the American context are destined to be frustrated and angry and to look on themselves as "oppressed." The irony, of course, is that America's multiethnic society and color-blind ideal—the equality of all citizens before the law—provides the most favorable setting for individuals to enjoy freedom and the opportunity to determine their destinies, even if they happen to be members of a minority. Ask Jews. For two thousand years Jews of the Diaspora have not been able to free their destiny from the power of gentiles. But in America they have done very well, thank you, and do not feel oppressed except, perhaps, by black demagogues like Farrakhan and company.

Politically Correct Jim Crow at Cornell University

You don't know what you're talking about. Do you know what kind of damage you're doing to your school? Do not come here next time." These were the words Cornell vice president Henrik Dullea used to several students during a private meeting about racially segregated dorms and clubs on the Ithaca campus. Dullea continued to harangue one particular student until she left with tears welling up in her eyes.

Why would a top-level administration member rebuke a student in such harsh and caustic terms? On most campuses, such a confrontation would be taboo, but for Cornellians, incidents like this one have become common as the university struggles with a growing racial polarization.

For the past few years, Cornell University has experienced a series of conflicts over the school's racially segregated dormitories. Under the guise of fostering an environment that is more multicultural and therefore theoretically more comfortable for minority students, the university has created several racial and ethnic living centers where these students can self-segregate. The first one was established in the wake of the infamous takeover of Cornell in 1969 by armed black students. The university erected a Latino living center in 1994 after student protesters stormed the administration building. A Native American living center exists as well.

The dorms may not yet have balkanized the campus into ethnic enclaves, but they have already sparked racial rancor and ethnic conflict. A student referendum revealed that nearly 60 percent of the student body opposed ethnic dormitories. The situation has become so sticky that, in May 1994, the New York Civil Rights Coalition and the New York Civil Liberties Union warned Cornell that they would challenge the segregated facilities if changes were not made.

"[Cornell] must not and will not be allowed to either institute or to perpetuate a system of Jim Crow facilities on the premise that students themselves say they prefer segregation," said Norman Siegel, executive director of the New York division of the American Civil Liberties Union, in a letter to President Frank Rhoades. Michael Meyers of the New York Civil Rights Coalition said that if Cornell did not dismantle this voluntary apartheid, he would file complaints with the New York Board of Regents and the U.S. Department of Education's Office of Civil Rights.

When notified of possible challenge to the dormitories by the New York Civil Rights Coalition and New York Civil Liberties Union, Henrik Dullea, the vice president of university relations, at first welcomed an inspection. "We have absolutely nothing to hide," he coolly declared. But when Siegel and Michael Meyers visited Cornell, they sensed that something was rotten in the state of New York. Rather than being reassured, the two men became even more determined to do something about the Ithaca campus, especially after talking to students who opposed the politically correct Jim Crow situation created by the administration. It was during the visit Siegel and Meyers made to Cornell, in fact, that Vice President Dullea issued the stinging rebuke that left several students stunned and one of them teary-eyed.

The meeting with Siegel and Meyers had been fairly placid until several students showed the two men anti-Semitic flyers that had been circulated by some residents of Ujaama, the all-black dormitory. That's when Dullea lost his cool and began to tongue-lash the students.

The episode was all the more surprising because Dullea is generally known as an affable and kind administrator. This has led observers to use the incident as a metaphor for the explosive atmosphere created on campus by the debate over multiculturalism. When asked later about his altercation with students, Vice President Dullea tried to downplay the incident. "There's no question that the students who met with Mr. Meyers and Mr. Siegel expressed themselves strenuously, and there were indeed disagreements," he said. "But I wouldn't characterize the meeting as explosive."

Dullea instead tried to conjure a more rosy picture of the meetings. "We took them [Siegel and Meyers] around campus and had them meet with students and faculty and staff who are involved with a variety of [ethnic] programs," he said. "I think they were good meetings. . . . Students involved in the program houses had an opportunity to tell why they felt they were very beneficial."

In fact, both men were appalled at what they saw. The New York Civil Liberties Union's Siegel said, "I understand [ethnic dorms] are a sensitive issue for the Cornell community, but I'm an integrationist and [the racial segregation] I saw today bothered me."

Meyers, of the New York Civil Rights Coalition, was more pointed in his reaction: "We went up [to Cornell] for an on-site inspection. There was no snow on the ground, but the university attempted to give us a snow job. It was not a convincing one. It's clear to me that there are segregated facilities with the complicity of the university, and it will be challenged."

Meyers implied that he felt he had been given a Potemkin Village tour. "Those who spoke with me were exclusively the ones the university apparently wanted me to talk to. They were only those who were supportive of theme houses," he said. "Sifting through all their explanations and rationalizations, I get the view that we were getting double-talk." Siegel was disturbed by the university's lack of cooperation: "We asked the school for information on the racial breakdown of Ujaama for the past twenty-two years, but we haven't gotten anything from the university."

Cornell has been embroiled in a long battle with the New York Board of Regents over these living arrangements. In 1978, the New York Board of Regents issued only a slap-on-the-wrist reprimand. But this time around, the board may not be as lenient. And that has worried many administration officials. (Although Cornell is known as a private Ivy League school, the university also has three state-supported colleges and is thus subject to many New York State regulations.)

Reaction on the Cornell campus to this incident has been mixed. The generally leftist bent of the New York Civil Liberties Union and the fact that the outspoken Michael Meyers is black have flustered many campus activists who would like to dismiss any mention of racial apartheid as a plot by white conservatives. "It's hard to understand why they would do such a thing. I would have expected right-wingers [to have challenged the dormitories] instead," one radical student remarked.

Even more interesting has been the splintering of the campus conservatives. Some conservative students are elated at the prospect of the ethnic houses being dismantled. "For years, student radicals have demanded special ethnic dormitories, and the university has willingly complied to their demands," said Michael Pulizotto, one of the students involved in the altercation with Vice President Dullea and a staff member of the conservative *Cornell Review*. "It is about time this kind of segregation and special treatment ends."

But other conservatives have watched the developments with apprehension, fearing that a state-mandated decision to dismantle segregated housing will allow other mandates on behalf of "more benign" affirmative action and multicultural programs in the future.

"This is yet another example of the Leviathan State assuming control of everything it touches," the *Cornell American* editorialized. "We neither want nor need the power of the State to support us in this fight because the right to private property is too important to compromise, even if doing so would seem to support our cause."

But campus radicals and conservatives alike are keeping their eyes on Michael Meyers, who has forthrightly expressed disgust over the new self-segregation that has insidiously crept into many universities. (The University of Michigan, for example, is home to "cultural lounges," which are restricted to use only by certain ethnic groups; and the University of California at Los Angeles offers separate commencement ceremonies for its minority students.) It is not surprising that Meyers, a lifelong NAACP member, would crusade for racial integration despite its current unpopularity among many members of the minority community.

While the NAACP and other civil rights leaders have coddled Louis Farrakhan, Meyers denounced the controversial Nation of Islam leader as an "apostle of hate" on the *MacNeil/Lehrer NewsHour*. "The so-called self-segregation will not be tolerated in any way," he said. "We have and will continue to challenge such segregation."

Meyers plans to challenge the segregated living facilities at Columbia University next. "As recipients of federal money, even [private schools are] under jurisdiction of the Civil Rights Office of the U.S. Department of Education," he says. "We have them [the schools] on the run, and we are very serious in ending the so-called self-segregation when the university has complicity in it."

It is ironic that this battle over the "new self-segregation" has occurred on the fortieth anniversary of *Brown v. Board of Education*. The landmark decision not only ruled that segregated public schools were unconstitutional but also challenged the racist ethos existing in America at the time. Ending this "new segregation" may be as painful and divisive as it was in Alabama forty years ago.

Black-on-White Crime

N ear midnight on Wednesday, December 29, 1992, a motorist discovered the body of a young woman alongside U.S. Highway 78 in Dorchester County near Charleston, South Carolina. She had been shot six times, with one bullet in her right arm and five more in her jaw. An autopsy would later determine that she had been shot at close range with a small-caliber firearm, the time of the shooting estimated to have been ten minutes before she was discovered. When found, she was still alive, but with weakening pulse and profuse bleeding. She died before help could arrive.

The young woman—Melissa McLauchlin, known as "Missy," twenty-five, a native of Wixom, Michigan, but living with her fiancé's family in North Charleston—was the victim of a brutal murder that was shocking enough, but the real shock would hit the Charleston area a few days later when two of her assassins were arrested. It was then revealed that Ms. McLauchlin was abducted, raped, tortured, and murdered—after being told beforehand that she would be killed—solely because of her race, by five black men. And the ultimate humiliation for the victim and her family was that the story of her murder would be curiously underplayed by the mainstream media—which, in cases where the racial identity of victim and perpetrator was reversed (as in the Tawana Brawley hoax), would blare out white guilt in banner headlines. The McLauchlin murder remained a local story despite the fact that the murderers' motivation—to "get a white girl" in revenge for "four hundred years of oppression"—made it the hate crime that the Tawana Brawley affair only pretended to be.

Some might say that the McLauchlin case, hideous though it was, was atypical and that the vast majority of hate crimes are committed by whites against blacks and other people of color. Yet recently released statistics from the Justice Department indicate that in 1993 about 1.3 million white Americans were the victims of violent crimes committed by blacks, as opposed to about 130,000 blacks who were victimized by whites. It is impossible to know how many of these crimes were motivated by explicit racial hatred, but it is clear that, adjusted for population, this means that blacks are responsible for fifty times more violent racial crimes than are whites.

The issue of black-on-white crime is the dirty little secret of American society—something almost everyone knows about or suspects, but no one discusses. To discuss it, in fact, is to run the risk of being stigmatized as a racist. Yet this is a problem that is worsening, particularly as a new generation comes of age. In the last twenty-eight years, violent crime has increased four times faster than the population, which means that a sizable segment of the population is working overtime committing crimes. It's no mystery that young people make up this segment. And black males under the age of eighteen are twelve times more likely than whites in the same age group to be arrested for murder.

According to the Justice Department's 1993 "Highlights from Twenty Years of Surveying Crime Victims," of the more than 6.6 million violent crimes committed annually in the United States (which are defined as rape, robbery, assault, and murder), about 20 percent are of an interracial nature. Most of the victims of these crimes—at least 90 percent—are white. According to the FBI's annual murder report, for instance, blacks murder whites at 18 times the rate that whites murder blacks. In gang-related assaults, violent black-on-white incidents are 21 times more likely to occur than the reverse. In gang robberies alone, whites are 52 times more likely to be victimized by blacks than the reverse. There are 7 times as many whites as blacks in the United States, yet a black is 12.38 times more likely to murder a white and 325 times more likely to participate in a gang attack on whites. And even by the most conservative estimate, a black man is 64 times more likely to rape a white woman than a white man is to rape a black woman.

Rape is the dirty little secret within the dirty little secret. As recently as the late 1950s, the vast majority of rapes were intraracial rather than interracial. By the 1970s, black-on-white rape was at least ten times more common than the reverse. (In 1974 in Denver, for example, 40 percent of all rapes were black-on-white, and there wasn't one reported case of white-on-black rape.) According to the respected criminologist William Wilbanks, in 1988 there were 9,406 reported cases of black-on-white rape, while there were fewer than 100 of white-on-black rape. And lest these figures be challenged as "conservative statistics," it should be noted that even Andrew Hacker, author of the impeccably liberal *Two Nations: Black and White, Separate, Hostile, Unequal*, admits that in 1989, blacks were three to four times more likely to commit rape than whites and that black men raped white women thirty times more frequently than white men raped black women.

Nor are the statistics the extent of the problem. As Dinesh D'Souza points out in *The End of Racism*, the racial character of rape has less to do with sexual thrills than with the desire to "control, dominate, and humiliate women," especially white women. Yet the fact that rape has become a predominantly black male crime is a reality that feminists, ever ready to decry our "rape culture," never seem to come to grips with, perhaps for fear of jeopardizing their tenuous bond with their black sisters. No politically correct feminist wants to point out the obvious: Transforming the "rape culture" in

America has far less to do with changing the mores of suburbia than with changing those of the ghetto.

What these statistics show is that the overwhelming majority of violent interracial crimes in America are not only committed by blacks against whites, but also occur every day with a predictability that is almost monotonous (except to the victims) and with something approaching complete apathy on the part of the media. It is not that the media are color blind. We hear a good deal about how blacks, especially young black males, are twice as likely to be killed as whites, although these are mostly black-on-black homicides. What about the equally obvious (for anyone who bothers to study the statistics) point that blacks kill twice as many whites as whites kill blacks? This is the hate crime that dare not speak its name, at least not on the polite airwaves or in the pages of the liberal press.

Were America the racist Reich that political correctness propagandists habitually paint it, the weight of these statistics would be reversed, and there might be some justification for the charges of "genocide" on the part of black activists and their white allies every time a posse of skinheads gets loose. But as author Jared Taylor points out, "Even a cursory search will bring to light little-known crimes committed by blacks against whites that would have been national news if committed by whites against blacks."

Consider the following rap sheet of crimes that were, with one or two exceptions, not deemed worthy of being treated as major stories:

One evening in July 1988, a young white man named Danny Gilmore of Warren, Ohio, was returning from the downtown Cleveland Rib Burn Off with two friends (who happened to be black) in his pickup truck. Lost, they were driving through a black East Side neighborhood, searching for the expressway on-ramp, when a black man on a moped pulled out into traffic without looking and bumped into them. Although the moped rider was unhurt (and at fault), Gilmore waited for the police to arrive. In the meantime, a crowd of young blacks, many of whom are believed to have been members of a local gang called the East Side Crushers, began to argue with Gilmore and his two friends and then attacked them. Gilmore was singled out. Hit on the head with a beer bottle, he collapsed onto the street in front of his truck. Gilmore was kicked and stomped by the gang, while one of them kept yelling, "Bum rush! Bum rush!"—a phrase taken from a popular rap song of the time, which they used as a code to designate their victims. Then one gang member jumped inside the cab of the truck, started the engine, and repeatedly ran Danny Gilmore over with his own vehicle while the assembled gangsters cheered. While Gilmore lay there crushed and helpless, one of the gang stole his wallet. Gilmore died the next day in a hospital without recovering consciousness. He was twenty-three.

The Cleveland establishment went out of its way to soft-pedal the racial angle of the Gilmore murder. Said the executive director of the city's Community Relations Board, Earl W. Williams, "As far as I'm concerned, it's not racial." Mr. Williams blamed the incident on a "pretty rough" neighborhood. The city's major newspaper, the *Plain-Dealer*, also downplayed race. In an irony that could occur only in the current political correctness climate, a black reporter for the paper who tried to cover the story in all its ramifications saw anxious white editors try to bury the racial angle.

One Cleveland homicide detective claimed, "The mayor's office doesn't want us to have racial killings in this town, so Danny Gilmore's death wasn't a racial crime. And I'm the tooth fairy."

A month after the widely reported Bensonhurst incident, which involved the shooting of a black youth by a member of a white gang, an almost identical crime was committed by blacks in the Bronx. A white man got out of his car to make a phone call on East Tremont Avenue, a racially mixed neighborhood. Two blacks approached and challenged him, "What are you white guys doing on Tremont? You don't belong here." There was an argument, and then one of the blacks pulled a gun and shot the white man in the stomach.

A prominent New York black activist minister, whose indignation over Bensonhurst had been widely quoted in the local press, said, "I don't know that that's racism as I define it. There's a difference between racism and revenge."

In October 1989, in Kenosha, Wisconsin, a group of young black men "hyped up" (in the words of one of them) with hate after viewing the film *Mississippi Burning,* with its depiction of Klan violence in the civil-rights-era South, determined to "move on some white people" and came upon fourteen-year-old Gregory Riddick, whom they beat savagely. The gang's leader, Todd Mitchell, received a sentence of four years: two years for aggravated battery, plus two more years for conducting a hate crime. Young Riddick was left with permanent brain damage.

One Saturday night in May 1990, in Tampa, a dozen black teens showed up at a local hangout frequented by white teens, looking for a fight, and got it. Trounced, they returned later with reinforcements. They found some of their recent opponents in a parking lot a few blocks away. They attacked the unarmed whites with clubs. One black pulled a pistol and fired, scattering the whites. The blacks then pursued one unfortunate kid for several blocks, finally cornering him. According to a woman who witnessed the result, seven blacks beat him with two-by-fours.

"I could see a piece of wood come down and crack against his head," she told police, adding that, with every blow, they roared: "Don't ever fuck with us! Don't ever fuck with us again!" The boy, aged nineteen, died; and four adults and two juveniles were charged with first-degree murder in his death.

In January 1991, in Boston, Robert Herbert and three other young black men made a pact to kill the first white person they saw. That hapless individual turned out to be Mark Belmore, a white student at Northeastern University, whom the foursome stabbed to death.

In San Diego, in December 1991, gangs of blacks went on "wilding" sprees, attacking forty-six white men and four white women, savagely beating them before robbing them. San Diego police refused to designate these offenses as hate crimes.

During 1991 and 1992, Hulon Mitchell, alias Yahweh ben Yahweh, leader of the Miami-based black "Hebrew" cult, the Yahweh Temple of Love, was tried on several counts of murdering, or having ordered the murders of, white people as ritual killings demanded of initiates of his cult. The Yahweh sect preached that the white man was, literally, the devil. As part of his indoctrination course in race hatred, Mitchell/ben Yahweh would show all members of his congregation—regardless of age or gender—pornographic films of white women having sex with either black men or animals as proof of "Miss Ann's" degraded, lustful nature. ("Miss Ann" was a common slave euphemism for the plantation's white mistress.)

Mitchell also taught classes in the proper procedure of killing white devils and demanded that their severed heads be brought back to him as proof. One sect member who obeyed his messiah's orders to kill three white devils and return with the trophies was former football player Robert Rozier. The first two devils he killed were his roommates, but since Rozier neglected to bring back their heads, Yahweh would not credit him with the kills. Rozier protested that toting a severed human head about town was not exactly inconspicuous behavior, so Yahweh eventually relented, allowing either a finger or an ear to fulfill the requirement.

Between 1986 and 1990, at least seven white people were known to have been dispatched by the Yahweh cultists, as were several blacks who made their enemies list. Miami police were reportedly reluctant to prosecute these murders out of fear that they would be denounced for persecuting a racial and religious minority, which was exactly the defense used by the Yahweh cult's attorney, former judge Alcee Hastings. Nonetheless, Mitchell was found guilty of conspiracy to commit murder.

On January 14, 1995, nineteen-year-old Michael Westerman of Guthrie, Kentucky, was murdered by a carload of blacks who were incensed by the Confederate flag flown from his pickup truck. Two eighteen-year-olds were sentenced to life in prison for the murder. Westerman is survived by a widow and an infant son.

On the afternoon of March 20, 1995, Valerie Johnson, 39, of Monessen, Pennsylvania, was walking down the street of her racially mixed neighborhood with her three-year-old son, Daniel. They passed by two black male teens who were talking. Their discussion was apparently peppered with the N-word, which Ms. Johnson's toddler innocently repeated.

Outraged, one of the African American youths hit Ms. Johnson in the face. Ms. Johnson apologized for her son's indiscretion and then returned home, where she called the police. Later that afternoon, Ms. Johnson and her son were walking near the local high school when she was set upon by the same two youths, Jason Stevenson, sixteen, and Vernon Majors, seventeen, along with an accomplice, Stevenson's brother James, nineteen. According to reports in local newspapers, Majors knocked her down and, as she tried to get up, James Stevenson kicked her in the face and head. After that she didn't move as Stevenson continued to kick her. His brother, Jason, pulled him away from her body, and the three escaped. A school superintendent saw Ms. Johnson lying upon the cement with her crying son standing beside her, wailing that a man had beat his mommy dead. An ambulance was called, which took her to a local hospital. There she was treated and released.

However, Ms. Johnson returned to the hospital the next day, and from there was transferred to two different Pittsburgh hospitals. In the last one she entered, on March 23, she died. The coroner's autopsy later determined that her death was at least partly due to blunt force injuries to the face.

The aftermath of Valerie Johnson's death produced the usual tragicomedy that occurs whenever black hate crimes take the life of a white victim. Friends and relations were at pains to assure the media that Valerie wasn't a racist, that she was friendly toward everyone in her racially mixed neighborhood, and that she would never have taught her son to use racial slurs such as the one that triggered her death.

The reactions of the black community were also typical. When seventeen-year-old Vernon Majors was arrested and taken before a magistrate for arraignment, a crowd of mostly teenage black girls gathered around police cars as he was led away, screaming their disapproval of this "racist" arrest. One woman was arrested for failing to disperse when ordered to do so. The crowd continued the protest across from the police station where Majors was temporarily held before being transferred to the county prison, shouting, "We love you, Vernon!"

For their part, the defendants were unrepentant. Majors, upon arraignment, asked, "How could you be charged for murder and all you did was push the babe?" He insisted that all he did was knock Johnson down from behind. As he ran away, he said he looked back to see the Stevenson brothers "finishing her." James Stevenson scoffed at the murder charges at his arraignment.

Later, during a preliminary hearing, Majors' cousin, Dana, testified that she witnessed the beating, substantiating her cousin's account of the Stevenson brothers kicking Valerie Johnson's fallen body. Ultimately her testimony was disregarded as biased in favor of Majors. Charges against James Stevenson and his sixteen-year-old brother, Jason, were dropped. On January 31, 1995, Majors was finally convicted of voluntary manslaughter and sentenced to a mere five years, less time already served.

As appalling as the preceding crimes are, none of them reached the moral squalor of the Melissa McLauchlin murder. In many of the other cases, even when premeditated, the violence was usually swift and decisive; in the McLauchlin case, the young woman was brutally degraded, humiliated, and sexually molested before she was heartlessly dispatched. More than a hate crime, it was a hate atrocity whose details read like a parable of black racial hate gone mad.

Four days after her body was found along the interstate, Melissa McLauchlin was identified by police. They had a victim. A day later, on January 3, 1993, they had their suspects—after seizing evidence from a trailer on Lot 3 of the Stall Road Mobile Home Park in North Charleston. Besides the county sheriff's office and the North Charleston police, a local newspaper reported, agents of the Naval Criminal Investigative Service were also involved since several of the suspects were current or former naval personnel.

The next day, two men were charged in what North Charleston police captain Charles Caldwell termed "a bad, bad crime." Arrested were Craig Rice, twenty-one, a sailor on the guided missile cruiser *Richmond K. Turner*, charged as an accessory-after-the-fact to murder, and Roger Williams, twenty-two, of the Stall Road trailer address, charged with misprision (withholding knowledge from police) of a felony and accessory to murder.

It was revealed that Melissa, who had been living with her boyfriend's family for over a year in North Charleston, quarreled with her boyfriend in a local nightclub; she left and began walking home. Ironically, a North Charleston police cruiser picked her up and took her home. However, she set off once more, supposedly for another area nightspot, but never arrived.

Not until two days after the crime was reported was it revealed that after leaving her boyfriend's home on the night of December 29, Melissa was lured into a car containing four or five men, taken to the trailer park home of several of them where she was gang-raped at gunpoint, and then taken back out in the car where she was shot and her body dumped alongside the highway several miles away. Police arrested another suspect, Danny Dwayne McCall, twenty-five, of North Charleston, and charged him with first-degree criminal sexual conduct and kidnapping. A first-degree sexual conduct charge was also brought against Roger Williams. Again, the suspects' race was not commented on in the press, but it was revealed that more suspects, including at least one woman, were being sought.

By January 7, six people had been arrested in Melissa McLauchlin's rape-murder. Added to the roll were Edna Jenkins, thirty, of North Charleston, charged with accessory-after-the-fact to murder

and kidnapping. Two suspects were arrested in hiding in Quaker-
town, Pennsylvania: Matthew Paul Williams, twenty-one, of the
Stall Road trailer home, a former sailor at Charleston Naval Base,
charged with murder, kidnapping, and first-degree sexual conduct,
and Indira Simmons, twenty-one, also of the Stall Road trailer park,
charged with accessory-after-the-fact to murder and criminal sexual
conduct and accessory-before-the-fact to kidnapping. Police said her
car was used to abduct Melissa; the murder also took place in the
car, and it was used to dispose of her body.

   With the additional arrests, more details concerning the incidents
of that awful night were revealed. Once Melissa was taken inside the
trailer, she was forced to strip and was tied up while she was raped by
six or seven men. While this went on, the two female suspects, girl-
friends of two of the men, were present in another room, apparently
aware of what was occurring but making no move to do anything
about it. After they were finished with her, the rapists decided that
they had to get rid of the evidence—meaning Melissa herself.
According to Captain Caldwell, Melissa was forced to shower and
was scrubbed with a nylon brush to remove traces of seminal fluid
and other evidence from her skin; then she was soaked in hydrogen
peroxide. The men then talked openly of their decision to kill
Melissa, letting her know that this was her fate. With her hands
bound behind her with toy handcuffs and a towel wrapped around
her head, Melissa was placed inside the car. Driven fourteen miles
out of town, she was shot five times in the head and once in the arm
while in transit; her body was dumped by the side of the interstate,
where she was discovered by a passing motorist not long after.

   At this point, nearly ten days after her murder, the racial vendetta
aspect of the Melissa McLauchlin case had still not been made
public. It would not come up until January 9, in the aftermath of the
arrest in Detroit of another fugitive suspect, Matthew Carl Mack,
twenty-one, also a former sailor from the *Richmond K. Turner* and a
resident of the Stall Road trailer home. Mack's capture left only one

suspect at large, Joe Gardner, twenty-two, petty officer second class aboard the *Richmond K. Turner* and, like Mack, a resident of the Stall Road trailer house. Gardner was believed to be the triggerman in Melissa's murder and ringleader in her abduction and rape; he was the object of a nationwide manhunt even as the whole sordid story of Melissa's murder was being revealed via the confession of Matthew Carl Mack.

McLauchlin, Mack asserted, was raped and kidnapped in retaliation for "400 years of oppression." The police had suspected a racial motivation when they found a "four-page document" at the trailer home crime scene, entitled "X-man." "It was a crudely written racial diatribe," filled with epithets about white oppression of blacks and blacks being "justified in seeking revenge," according to one police detective who examined it.

Even so, police were reluctant to brand the McLauchlin murder as a hate crime. "I think we have to be responsible to the community and the people we protect," Captain Caldwell cryptically explained. "I didn't want to believe this was a racial crime. And we tried to look for other motivations."

It seems unlikely that such cautious sifting of theories would be tolerated in a case involving, say, the burning of a black man by two white youths, to cite an actual case that happened in the same week as McLauchlin's murder only a few hundred miles south in Tallahassee. Nationwide, the press showcased that murder as a typical hate crime: one perpetrated by vicious white racists against an innocent black. President Clinton mentioned the Tallahassee burning in his State of the Union address as an example of the sort of violent racism that still needed to be expunged from the American character. Neither the national press nor the president mentioned Melissa McLauchlin.

The Charleston police reported that several of the suspects in Melissa's case told them repeatedly the same story: that they had decided on December 29, 1992, as a sort of "New Year's resolution," to kidnap a white woman, rape her, and then kill her. It wasn't long after these revelations that leaders of Charleston's black community weighed in with their outraged objections, particularly South Carolina state senator Robert Ford, a Democrat from Charleston. Ford doubted that the crime was an act of racial hate.

Police Captain Caldwell then admitted that the reason for his previous reluctance to emphasize the McLauchlin case as a hate crime was because of the possible repercussions within the community. In essence, he was wary of sparking a racial conflagration. Melissa's fiancé, John Owen, also felt that she was targeted because of her skin color.

On January 12, the prosecutors in the McLauchlin case announced their intention "to seek the death penalty on whoever shot this girl." At this time, the case had still failed to generate much national attention. The story was not handled by the major networks, the two major newsmagazines, *Time* and *Newsweek*, or the two major national newspapers, the *New York Times* and the *Washington Post*.

On February 17, the McLauchlins appeared on a *Montel Williams* episode entitled "They Killed My Daughter Because She Was White." No other television show was interested.

On May 22, 1994, nearly seventeen months after her death, the trial of Melissa McLauchlin's murderers began. The first defendant to be tried for murder, with the death penalty sought by prosecutors, was Matthew Carl Mack. The circus began when defense attorney Peter Them accused the media of issuing "grossly inflammatory and factually dishonest" reports. He also accused the police of manipulating the racial issue by continuing to "dribble out provocative and false information to the media."

In the meantime, in Detroit, police raided the home of Joe Gardner's parents. They discovered the car in which Melissa had been killed and a bloody shirt presumed to belong to Gardner. Police told the *Detroit Free Press* that Gardner's mother, a Wayne County deputy sheriff, was "not helpful" in the search for her son. On May 26, on the eve of the murder trials of his brothers-in-crime (it was determined to try Matthew Williams in a separate trial from Matthew Carl Mack), Joe Gardner was placed on the FBI's "Ten Most Wanted" list.

The jury chosen to try Mack consisted of five white women, five white men, and two black women. One black woman was released from duty: She became hysterical mere minutes after being selected. She told the judge she hadn't been able to sleep since initial questioning and was suffering from migraines. In a random draw, she was replaced by a white man.

With no question of their guilt and no moral justification for their actions, the defendants and their attorneys embarked on the ultimately self-defeating strategy of defaming their victim's character.

Roger Williams testified that Melissa was "tricking for crack cocaine." He claimed that he was summoned to Mack's trailer by Matthew Williams to help in a fight. When he got there, he was told that there was a girl present who was exchanging sex for drugs. He claims he was told to pretend to be the guy with the drugs in return for having sex with her. He claimed his sex was consensual, and so was Mack's, as he was present when it took place.

He also claimed that Gardner grew angry with Melissa, screamed at her, then tried unsuccessfully to penetrate her anally. Williams tried to calm Gardner, which he said made Gardner angry enough to throw him out. He claimed that he did not know that Gardner had killed McLauchlin until the next day.

Indira Simmons, Matthew Williams's girlfriend, testified that she was in the trailer that night; she lived with Williams and Mack. Williams told her that the other guys had a prostitute in another room. She claimed to have seen McLauchlin in the kitchen and that she smiled and did not seem distressed. She said that Mack came into her room later holding a knife, claiming that "he was going to kill the bitch." She said she thought he was kidding.

Edna Jenkins, Gardner's girlfriend at the time, said she got to the trailer about the time Roger Williams was leaving. She claimed to overhear Gardner, Mack, and Matthew Williams discussing something urgent, saying things like "What you gonna do? We got to do that."

Just before she left, she saw those same men bring a woman from the trailer, with a scarf covering her face and her hands tied behind her back. She said she didn't know what the men were up to until the next day.

For his part, Mack claimed that he thought Melissa was going to be dropped off unharmed until Gardner suddenly shot her five times in the head with a pistol at close range.

All three witnesses, of course, cut deals with the prosecution in exchange for their testimony. Prosecutor Bailey conceded that Melissa voluntarily entered the car with the five black men but could not have known their intentions. He did not say on what evidence he based his belief, since the victim was not present to contradict any of the testimony, but this concession may have been part of the deal he cut with the three defendants who testified as prosecution witnesses.

Melissa's boyfriend and fiancé, John Owen, admitted that Melissa had had a drug problem when they had lived in Florida but said that she had cleaned up. And contrary to defense allegations about Melissa's drug use that last night of her life, her autopsy revealed that, while there was evidence of alcohol in her system, there were no traces of drugs.

The most damaging witness against Mack was his next-door neighbor, Pamela Holt, who testified that Mack asked her, the day after Melissa's death, if she had been watching the news lately. When Holt asked why, Mack told her "We killed a white bitch last night. We've been planning on doing this for a while." He then gave her this account:

On the night of December 29, 1992, Mack, Matthew Williams, and Joe Gardner were riding around when they saw McLauchlin, obviously drunk, walking alongside the road. She asked them if they wanted to party and if they had any "rock" (crack). They told her they didn't and started to leave, but McLauchlin "called them niggers and stuff, and threw rocks at the car."

They stopped, told McLauchlin that they did have drugs, but that she would have to come back to their trailer to get them. She then got in the car with them, voluntarily. But when she got there, and found out that they had lied about the drugs, she refused to have sex with anyone.

Then "Joe [Gardner] put the gun to her head and said, 'take off all your clothes.' Joe took her back in the front room and raped her."

When it was all over, Melissa was told to scrub herself off with hydrogen peroxide, and Mack scrubbed her down with a steel wool pad. Then she was blindfolded with a towel, her hands confined behind her back with toy handcuffs. She was put into the back seat of the car with Williams.

During the ride, Melissa "was doing a lot of screaming and kicking; [Williams] was punching her, trying to shut her up." At this point, Gardner turned around and shot her.

Williams expressed shock and asked Gardner why he had done that. "I thought we were just going to strangle her and throw her in the woods!"

Taking the witness stand in his own defense, Mack claimed that Gardner brought up the idea of killing Melissa because "she kept demanding drugs or money after willingly having sex with them."

Mack had earlier told police that he was mad at his former white girlfriend a day or so before the McLauchlin murder when he told Gardner and Matthew Williams that he'd like to strangle her.

According to a Detroit police homicide report, made after his arrest there, Mack said that "any white girl would do," but also claimed, "we were just sitting around joking."

Mack testified that it was Gardner who made Melissa shower to cleanse away incriminating evidence, Gardner who blindfolded her and then bound her with toy handcuffs. He quoted Gardner as saying, "Man, we're going to have to kill that bitch."

Mack insisted that there was no plot between himself, Gardner, and Matthew Williams to abduct, rape, torture, and kill a white girl, that the alleged motive was made up by the police, who combined three unrelated statements made over the course of two hours to make it look like a plot. However, Mack was contradicted by a tape recording of his own voice.

In that tape, Mack related that he, Gardner, and Williams had been drinking all day and watching movies, including one pornographic movie dealing with interracial sex and two of the *Faces of Death* movies, which show real deaths and executions. It was during these viewings that Mack, angry at his white girlfriend, made the remark that he wanted to kill her, even "stab her," but conceded that "it ain't got to be her, any white" would do.

And as they watched the pornographic film, involving a black man and a white woman, Williams allegedly expressed his desire to have a white woman. About two hours later, they were watching a TV news show recapping the biggest stories of the year (1992), prominent among which was the videotaped beating of Rodney King by several white Los Angeles police officers. This caused Gardner to exclaim, "That's four hundred years of oppression!" Gardner went on to say that his New Year's resolution was "to kill a white bitch."

In another statement that Mack made to naval investigators, but that he denied making at the trial, Mack remembered asking Williams: "How many years do you think this takes off the oppression of the black race?" Williams replied, "About ten years."

In his summary, Prosecutor Bailey pointed out that all accounts showed that nobody had sex with Melissa until after Gardner pulled a gun on her, that even Mack, insisting that McLauchlin had consensual sex with him, admitted that although she didn't say "no," she cried and pleaded with him not to hurt her. "Does that sound like consensual sex to any of you?" he inquired of the jurors.

The jury, eleven whites and one black, answered by giving Mack life imprisonment plus thirty years for the kidnapping and murder of

Melissa McLauchlin. But they rejected the state's plea for the death penalty. Under the life sentence, Mack will be eligible for parole after serving thirty years, in 2024.

Matthew Williams received the same sentence. Indira Simmons, Edna Jenkins, and Roger Williams all copped pleas.

On October 20, 1994, Joe Gardner, the man who shot Melissa McLauchlin, was finally arrested by the FBI in Philadelphia, where he was working as a grocery clerk under an alias. "We wanted this fellow very badly," noted Dorchester County Sheriff Sutherland, who said there were many smiles and cheers in his office when the news came through.

On April 14, 1995, Gardner pleaded not guilty. Prosecutors asked for the death penalty. On December 10, 1995, Gardner was convicted of the kidnapping and murder of Melissa McLauchlin by a jury of seven women and five men. They returned their decision after only two hours of deliberation. On December 13, the same jury took another two hours to decide that Joe Gardner should forfeit his life in the electric chair or by lethal injection.

The McLauchlin murder was a wedge driven between the black and white communities in the Charleston area, threatening initially to erupt into racial conflict. This is reflected in letters sent to the city's largest newspaper, the *Post and Courier*. White readers in particular were outraged that certain members of the black community's leadership, like State Senator Ford, were trying to downplay any suggestion that the McLauchlin murder was a case of black racism and were accusing the media of sensationalizing, if not inventing, that angle. Several white readers complained, again and again, in nearly the same words in each letter, that had the skin colors of the victim and her murderers been reversed, there would have been no end to the hue and cry from professional "anti-racist" groups like the NAACP, ACLU, Southern Poverty Law Center, and Center for Democratic Renewal, all of whom were noticeably mute during the days that the McLauchlin story took center stage in Charleston.

Many white readers bitterly pointed out the inadequacy of the national news media's coverage of the McLauchlin murder in comparison to the urgency with which they treated white-on-black incidents. One reader wondered why there was so little interest in the case from the federal level. "Where are the U.S. Justice Department and the Attorney General's office to look into violations of her civil rights?" he asked. "When this tragic event is compared to some of the petty events in which there have been questions of civil rights and racial prejudice in the Charleston area in the past six months, there is no comparison in their harshness."

There were contrary white views. One thirty-one-year-old woman, a former teacher, wrote a long letter in which she urged the Charleston area to "get a grip" on itself. After speaking of African Americans' contribution to the culture of Charleston, she pointed out that all the serial killers she ever heard of were white and that most murder victims were killed by someone of the same skin color. Such reflexively self-righteous letters as this one highlighted the nervousness that Melissa's case engendered among white liberals. Another woman reader played the feminist card and pointed out that the McLauchlin murder was only 50 percent racially motivated "since the suspects stated that they were looking for a white woman victim. . . . Therefore the crime was 50 percent gender motivated." For her, "sensationalizing the rape/murder as 100 percent racially motivated adds to already serious racial tensions and downplays the importance of rape as a crime of hate against women."

Senator Robert Ford retaliated against his critics, chiding "decent white people" for remaining silent whenever racist outrages were perpetrated against blacks. Ford even implied that the police should be investigated for possibly inventing a racist plot in the McLauchlin case. At the same time, he congratulated the police for their swift apprehension of the perpetrators but opined that it would have taken two weeks or more, rather than a mere forty-eight hours, for the police to make any arrests if McLauchlin had been a black woman.

One black reader defended the NAACP and black leaders, after making the obligatory murmurs of outrage against "the eight 'sleaze bags' who committed the alleged crime." It was this phrase that outraged Leonard Singleton, who would have been Melissa's father-in-law, into responding, "How can he possibly say the 'alleged' crime? Does he think that it did not happen? . . . Imagine your mother, wife, sister, or your girlfriend being kidnapped and raped at gunpoint by six men, while two women were there. Imagine being tortured and told you are going to die. Imagine just what Missy went through the last two hours of her life. Let each one of the suspects be tried on what they did to Missy."

Some will say that, in fact, the media do report on black hate crimes and even overemphasize them, members of the media being predominantly white. They will point to the Central Park jogger "wilding" of 1988; the black riots against Hasidic Jews in Crown Heights, Brooklyn, which resulted in the stabbing death of Yankel Rosenbaum in 1991; the near-fatal gang beating of white truck driver Reginald Denny during the South Central Los Angeles riots; the shooting of a white congressman's aide by a black man who vowed to kill a white in Washington, D.C., in 1992; Jamaican immigrant Colin Ferguson's massacre of white and Asian commuters on the Long Island Railroad in 1993; or the shooting of three-year-old Stephanie Kuhen by members of a Chicano gang when her father turned down the wrong street in Los Angeles last year.

Members of the press do tend to notice things that happen in their own backyards, in cities where media or governmental power resides. But incidents that occur in the rest of the country may as well have happened on Mars for all the coverage they are granted. The McLauchlin murder alone should have been a major media issue, the kind that leads to the sort of national soul searching that the Tawana Brawley hoax elicited. But it wasn't. So many black-on-white crimes just don't qualify for marquee billing.

This peculiar tendency to overlook, downplay, excuse, or even justify anti-white hate crimes only seems to embolden some prominent blacks to admit to their own (hopefully) former tendency to indulge in such activity. One would think that this sort of confession would be held against the confessors, or at least would damage their career prospects, as it would for any white writers who confessed to having beaten up blacks for kicks while a skinhead or junior Klansman. Far from it; it actually seems to be a career enhancement for young black males seeking to establish their street credibility in certain political correctness/diversity enclaves. Consider the acclaim that greeted *Washington Post* writer Nathan McCall's autobiography, *Makes Me Wanna Holler: A Young Black Man in America*. In this memoir, which was widely praised with words like "unflinching honesty," McCall begins with the account of a beating he and his friends inflicted upon a hapless teenage white boy who made the mistake of riding his bicycle through their neighborhood.

"He was definitely in the wrong place to be doing the tourist bit," McCall blithely recalls. He says that he took out after the kid along with his pals. Catching up with him, they knocked him off his bike. "He fell to the ground and it was all over. We were on him like white on rice. Ignoring the passing cars, we stomped and kicked him. My stick partners kicked him in the head and face and watched the blood gush from his mouth. I kicked him in the stomach and nuts, where I knew it would hurt. Every time I drove my foot into his balls, I felt better, with each blow delivered I gritted my teeth as I remembered some recent racial slight."

The white boy had curled up into a fetal position trying to protect his head and vitals. McCall claims that he and the rest backed off, fearing that they had killed him, "but one dude kept stomping, like he'd gone berserk. He seemed crazed and consumed in the pleasure of kicking that white boy's ass. When he finished, he reached down and picked up the white dude's bike, lifted it as high as he could above his head, and slammed it down on him hard." McCall knew the boy was still alive only because he was breathing; otherwise, the boy didn't even flinch when the bike was slammed down on him; he was out cold. McCall and his friends left laughing and boasting about what they had done.

McCall relates how "good" it made him and his friends feel to bumrush white boys, getting revenge on behalf of all black people. They called it "gettin' some get-back." McCall remembers that after his older brother got his driver's license, his gang would cruise into white neighborhoods, looking for pedestrians to assault. "Using sticks and fists," he recalls, they would then "beat them to within an inch of their lives."

Now, from his comfortable vantage point as a successful journalist with a major establishment newspaper, McCall can look back on it all; and while distancing himself from all those "crazy things the fellas and I did and . . . the hate and violence that we unleashed," he can still justify it when he considers the way white America has treated blacks: "Our random rage in the old days makes perfect sense to me."

There are several revealing passages later in McCall's book that shed some ironic significance on his violent past. At one point, musing on the departure of one of his few white friends at work, McCall muses, "It's sad this, this gulf between blacks and whites. We're so afraid of each other." While McCall spends most of the book excoriating whites for everything he can think of, it never seems to occur to him that his own past behavior has contributed to this gulf. Whites afraid of him? Gosh, wonder why? At another point, he tells of the time when he confronts the new multiculturalist editor with information that he has served time for armed robbery. The editor blandly replies, "Is that all?" and tells him to let him know if anyone gives him "shit" about it.

With writers like McCall on staff at major papers, in concert with those editors who hire and pamper them, it's no wonder that antiwhite hate crimes like the rape-murder of Melissa McLauchlin are censored from the pages of papers like McCall's own domain, the *Washington Post,* and remain the best-known but least-discussed social problem in America.

CONTRIBUTORS

K. L. BILLINGSLEY is a journalism fellow at the Center for the Study of Popular Culture and author of *The Generation That Knew Not Joseph*, a book about the religious Left.

KATE COLEMAN has written for *Newsweek* and now works as a freelance journalist in the Bay Area. She is completing a biography of former Black Panther leader Huey Newton.

G. J. KRUPEY is a freelance writer specializing in music and social issues. He lives and works in Pennsylvania.

KENNETH LEE has written for *American Enterprise* and other magazines and has worked on the editorial staff of *The New Republic*.

PAUL MULSHINE has worked for the *Philadelphia Daily News* and is now a columnist for the *Star Ledger* in Newark, New Jersey.

DEROY MURDOCK is a New York–based syndicated columnist who appears on the MSNBC network.

WARD PARKS is a professor of English at Louisiana State University. In addition to writing for *Heterodoxy*, he has published pieces in various scholarly publications.

HUGH PEARSON has written editorials for the *Wall Street Journal*. He is the author of *The Shadow of the Panther*, a history of the rise and fall of the Black Panther Party.

CRISTOPHER RAPP has written numerous articles on social issues for *Heterodoxy*. He is the managing editor for the publication *Fathers and Families*.

MATTHEW ROBINSON is a staff writer for *Investor's Business Daily*.

INDEX